RABBIS AND VEGETARIANISM: AN EVOLVING TRADITION

Editor: Roberta Kalechofsky

micah publications, inc.

Rabbis and Vegetarianism: An Evolving Tradition, Copyright (c), 1995 by Micah Publications, Inc.

All rights reserved. Except for use covered under the Fair Use Clause in the Copyright Law, no portions of this book may be reproduced without permission from the publisher. Send inquiries to Micah Publications, Inc., 255 Humphrey St., Marblehead, MA 01945 (617-631-7601).

General Editor: Roberta Kalechofsky
Production Editors: Robert and Roberta Kalechofsky
Printed in the United States of America

ISBN: 916288-42-0

Acknowledgements, with permission from publisher and/or author:
Rabbi David Brusin, "Eating Meat May Be Contrary to Judaism," Wisconsin Jewish Journal, June 12, 1987.
Rabbi Arthur Green, excerpts from Seek My Face, Speak My Name, permission of publisher, Jason Aronson, Inc., Northvale, NJ (c) 1992.
Rabbi Sidney J. Jacobs, excerpts from Jewish Clues to Your Health and Happiness, permission of author and publisher, Jacobs Ladder Publications, 1990.
Rabbi Edward Rosenthal, "Ethical Vegetarianism: The Perspective of a Reform Jew, Reform Jewish Quarterly, Spring, 1992.
Rabbi Zalman Schachter-Shalomi, Foreward to Vegetarianism and the Jewish Tradition, by Louis Berman, Ktav Pub. House, 1982.
Rabbi Harold Schulweis, "Thou Shalt Eat Vegetables," Reform Judaism, Summer 1995, vol. 23, no. 4.
Writings of Rabbis Chaim Maccoby, Sidney Clayman, Chaim Chezkiyahu Medini, and David Rosen: "New Year Message, 1988," "The Torah and Flesh Eating," "On the Temple Sacrifices," The International Jewish Vegetarian Newsletter, 855 Finchley Road, London NW11 8LX, England.
Rabbi Noach Valley, "I Know I Shouldn't, But I do It Anyway," The North American Jewish Vegetarian Newsletter, Fall, 1992.

micah publications, inc.

CONTENTS

Rabbi Abraham Kook,
From "A Vision of Vegetarianism and Peace": 1
Rabbi David Brusin,
Eating Meat May Be Contrary to Judaism: 7
Rabbi Sidney Clayman,
Vegetarianism: The Ideal of The Bible: 9
Rabbi Stephen Fuchs,
Enhancing The Divine Image: 13
Rabbi Everett Gendler,
The Universal Chorus: 18
Rabbi Arthur Green,
From Seek My Face, Speak My Name: 23
Rabbi Sidney J. Jacobs,
To Your Health: 28
Rabbi Bonnie Koppell,
Vegetarianism: 37
Rabbi Emily Faust Korzenik,
Kashrut For the 21st Century: 40
Rabbi Michael Kramer,
A Personal Statement: 44
Rabbi C.Z. Maccoby,
The Kamenitzer Maggid: 47
Rabbi Chaim C. Medini,
Extract from Sdei Chemed: 50
Rabbi David Rosen,
An Orthodox Jewish Perspective: 53
Rabbi Edward Rosenthal,
Ethical Vegetarianism: 61
Rabbi Zalman Schachter-Shalomi,
Foreword to Vegetarianism & the Jewish Tradition: 75
Rabbi Harold Schulweis,
"Thou Shalt Eat Vegetables": 80
Rabbi Noach Valley,
"I Know I Shouldn't, But I Do It Anyway": 86

Glossary   90
Biographical Notes   94

Introduction

In the last hundred years there has been a growing rabbinic sentiment for Jewish vegetarianism, which will influence the concepts of kashruth. The traditional Jewish attitude towards meat is expressed by an historic tension between God's concession towards the human desire for meat, and what Rabbi Arthur Green rightly points to as the "provegetarian bias" in Torah. While a concession to eat meat was granted to Noah, it was granted with a curse, and meat gluttony is condemned throughout the Hebrew Bible; Adam and Eve were created as vegetarians; the seven sacred foods of the biblical Jew (olives, grapes, pomegranates, dates, wheat, barley, honey) do not include meat; and in a religion rich in blessings for foods, there is no blessing for meat. Talmudic statements, such as "Man should not teach his son to eat meat" (Chullin 84a) are numerous; finally, the Messianic world, as was the Edenic world, is envisioned as vegetarian.

In addition to the rabbis in this anthology, statements by other rabbis abound. Rabbi Shlomo Riskin has been a frequent contributor to the growing sentiment for Jewish vegetarianism, often using the occasion of the Shabbbat Noah portion to point out that Genesis sets the stage for vegetarianism, and to expand on the teachings of Rav Kook. In The Jerusalem Post (Nov. 16, 1993), he wrote, "May the time soon arrive when...the only use of knives will be for slicing hallah to be eaten with milk and honey--not meat--in honor of Sabbath and festivals." Rabbi Harold Kushner, in his book, To Life, wrote:

> "The major Jewish dietary laws rest on a single premise: *Eating meat is a moral compromise.* There is a difference between eating a hamburger and eating a bowl of cereal. For one of them, a living creature had to be killed. Should we ever become so casual about the eating of meat that we lose sight of that distinction, a part of our humanity will have shriveled and died."

A quiet revolution is taking place in the millennial tradition of kashruth, whose vegetarian sentiment has been fermenting throughout Jewish history. The "provegetarian bias" was recognized and explored throughout the centuries by the Nazaritic tradition, Kabbalistic mystics, Essenes, and the Karaites who banned meat-eating in the tenth century (but, alas! became backsliders). By the late 19th and early 20th centuries, the "provegetarian bias" became a prominent theme, as evidenced by the writings of Rabbi Medini, Rev. Chaim Maccoby, and Rav Kook. More contemporarily, a confluence of reasons based on revulsion towards modern husbandry, the Holocaust, and the felt need to move away from all expressions of violence, motivate the Jewish vegetarian movement.

The articles in this anthology are arranged alphabetically, except for Rabbi Kook's writings, which are excerpted from a lecture called "Chalutzim of the Messiah," based on his book, <u>A Vision of Vegetarianism and Peace.</u> Rav Kook's position among Jewish religious vegetarians is exemplary. His writings touch on most of the themes in which Jewish vegetarian arguments are grounded: Edenic vegetarianism, the meaning of "dominion" in Genesis, the concession to Noah and humankind's "lust for meat," the commandment to cover the blood, the commandment not to seethe a kid in its mother's milk and its further development to separate milk and meat, the laws of shechitah, and the sense that an historical moment has come in the history of the Jewish diet.

These are the themes in the articles in this anthology. Our commentators see in the laws of kashruth a "concession to meat eating" and, paradoxically, the strategy for limiting meat-eating. However, while kashruth may have achieved that limitation in the past, modern habits of eating meat have broken down the balance between "concession" and "limitation." Modern Jews in the West, like most westerners, eat as much meat as they can, even if it is kosher meat; and as Rabbi Kushner warns against, have, for all intents and purposes, lost the distinction between eating a living creature and eating a bowl of cereal. Modernity has proven a formidable foe of kashruth, making it all but impossible for kashruth and shechitah to function meaningfully in the way that they were historically meant to function. In his essay, Rabbi David Rosen declares that it is nothing less than a *Chillul Hashem* (desecration of the Name of God) to declare veal to be kosher; that modern methods of factory farming flout the Jewish teachings of tsa'ar ba'alei chayim; and states that it is no longer legitimate for Jews to eat meat. Rabbi Shalomi-Schachter asks, "Can a substance at the same time be kosher and dangerous to human health?" pointing to the multitudinous chemicals, pesticides and hormones used in today's meat which make the animal's life barbarous and unhealthy for humans to consume. The traditionally honorable systems of kashruth and shechitah cannot barricade themselves behind technicalities much longer and still be honorable. There is a felt need for a change to a Jewish diet exemplified by vegetarianism that would be more consonant with Judaism's principles.

The contributors to this volume approach the prospect in individual ways. Not all became vegetarians in the same way; some are aspiring vegetarians; some were "accidental" vegetarians; some, like Rabbi Emily Faust Korzenik, were influenced by their children; some emphasize the value of human health (pikuach nefesh) in vegetarianism; others, like Rabbi Everett Gendler, the value of creaturely kinship and the concern for animal life (tsa'ar ba'alei chayim); others, like Rabbi Green, believe that Jewish vegetarianism is a fundamental principle in a "theology of creation." Whatever the originating impulse towards vegetarianism was, all agree that Jewish vegetarianism is an historic development in Jewish history, that it intensifies one's sense of holiness, one's awareness of all creation, and the magnanimity of the Creator of all life.

Roberta Kalechofsky
September, 1995
Tishri 5756

A Vision of Vegetarianism And Peace

Rabbi Yitzchak HaCohen Kook
Edited and Compiled by Rabbi David HaCohen: A Lecture by Joe Green

The Religious Vegetarians

Somewhere, some time during the last century, there existed a group of individuals whose outlook on life bore the stamp of infinite glory in that they foresaw a period in history when man would ascend to such a high level of conduct, that he would live in peace not only with his fellow-man, but with the beast in the field and the cattle in the stall.

They were the Religious Vegetarians.

Modern Jewish historians make no mention at all of them. Were it not for that most noble of men, that saint above saints, the Nazeer of Jerusalem, Rabbi David HaCohen, their names and their teachings would have disappeared into the limbo of forgotten things.

This great man almost single-handedly held aloft the torch of their doctrines in the midst of a world of violence and confusion. He did more than that. Dipping his pen in ink made indelible with its cultural and ethical content, he recorded for all time the opinions of their inspired leader, Rabbi Yitzchak HaCohen Kook, in a volume entitled "The Vision of Vegetarianism and Peace."

For this the "Nazeer" will be hailed in days to come as the man who preserved and handed on the noblest tradition of them all, the concept of compassion that extends to all living things--be it man, fowl, or beast.

An examination of the contents of the booklet is startling in the extreme, for not only does it preach compassion, but it affirms in no uncertain terms that the final objective of Judaism is a world without slaughter or pain--that is, a vegetarian one.

The Rights of Animals

The Rabbi commences his work without any preliminaries. He states that man in his upward journey has overlooked one cardinal factor, and that is the rights of animals. This, he declares, is due to the fact that man has adopted philosophies of life that make no provision for the rightful treatment of animals. "However, not all the sophistry in the world can strangle that innate deep-seated feeling of righteousness that the Lord has implanted in the heart of man. With regard to animals, it exists as a hardly discernible spark which lies buried beneath a heap of ash. *It is a great shortcoming in man's spiritual make-up that he does not give full play to this goodly and noble feeling which in effect entails the non-slaughter of living creatures for man's needs and pleasures....*"

Man And His Dominion

"There can be no doubt in the minds of every thinking man that the concept of dominion as expressed in the Torah--(They shall have supreme power over the fish of the sea, over the birds of the heavens and all living things that move upon the Earth)--does not in any way imply the rule of a haughty despot who tyrannically governs his people and his servants for his own personal selfish ends and with a stubborn heart. Heaven forfend that such a repulsive form of servitude be forever integrated (sealed) in the world of the Lord, whose tender mercies are on all His work, of whom it is said, 'He shall build a world of kindness.' And what is more, the Torah already testifies that there was once a time when mankind had the courage to raise itself to a high moral level. The Sages in their writings and their commentaries demonstrated that the first man (Adam) was not permitted to regard meat as food--(Behold I have given you every tree yielding seed for food). It was only after the flood, in the days of Noah, that it was permitted to them (i.e. meat as food). 'Even as the green herb I have given you all.'

Is it therefore possible to conceive that a virtue of such priceless value, which had at one time been in fact a possession of mankind, should be lost forever?

Because of this it is said, 'I will fetch my knowledge from afar and I will render righteousness to my Maker.' The future will expand our tread (quicken our pace) and will extricate us from this complicated problem."

By this the Rabbi meant that at some time in the future mankind's ideas would change and that he would search far and wide for a solution to this and other problems, and when the solution was discovered, he would hasten with quickened steps to render righteousness to the Lord.

The Lust For Meat

"When permission was granted in the Torah to eat meat, 'You shall say, You shall eat meat because your soul eagerly desires to eat meat. You will eat meat with all the longing of your soul.'---In this statement is concealed a shrewd reproach and a qualified injunction---It was not necessary for the Torah to legislate against the eating of human flesh, as a detestation for this had already become part of man's moral creed. In the same way there will come the day when man will detest the eating of the flesh of animals because of the moral loathing entailed therein. Then it shall be said: Because your soul does not long to eat meat, you will not eat meat.

The Ethical Decline

"Animals too will have to pay the price of transition---just as mankind will have to make great sacrifices on the altar of human perfection. But the glorious future will wipe away all tears, as it is written, 'and the Lord shall wipe away the tears from all faces.'

It is evident that because of man's frailty which itself stems from his ethical decline, he was able to adapt himself to the eating of meat. Even so, in this very permission which came into effect after the flood (permitting meat to be used for food), there is contained within the depths of the Torah a logical deduction that such a consent could not be applicable to the end of time. For how is it possible to change such a high standard of conduct [as existed in Eden], especially when such had already been the custom?...."

Wool

The Rabbi states in clear terms that the utilization of the natural possessions and products of animals must be viewed in accordance with the light of divine compassion that is implicitly in the Torah.

Wool and milk are the natural possessions of the animals concerned, but man "in his weakness and his love for himself oversteps all boundaries, approaches the humble cow and the unfortunate sheep and takes from one its milk and from the other its wool.

Such action is not in accordance with the logical deduction that will stem from the fulfillment of the Torah concept--the objects of which are to strengthen the knowledge of the ways of the Lord, to enhance the glory of His Name and (to proclaim) that He will rule through the power of Divine Love.

It is worthy to note that no moral blemish is entailed if the wool is removed from the sheep at a time when the owner of the wool (the sheep) has his burden lightened thereby, or no harm results to him. It is a different matter if one takes the wool for one's own needs at a time when the natural owner (the sheep) is itself in need thereof. This can only be construed as robbing the animal of its just rights."

Milk

Similarly, the Rabbi discusses the question of milk. He likens the taking of milk to the taking of the animal's life and the flesh from it. "Milk was destined to feed the animal's offspring and not that man should take it with force for himself. The kid has the right to enjoy its mother's milk and its mother's love, but hard-hearted man, influenced by his materialistic and shallow outlook, changes and perverts these true functions (concepts). Thus the gentle kid is unable to partake of its mother's love and rejoice in the splendor of life. He is slaughtered and becomes food for man's gluttonous stomach. Now what will be the function of the milk but to cook the slaughtered kid in it, for this is a natural combination of these two elements.

But, 'Son of Man,' give ear to that which calls behind you. It is the voice of the Lord crying out to you with vigour: *You shall not seethe the kid in its mother's milk.* The destiny of the kid is not to become food to be ground by your sharp teeth. Milk was never intended to be a spice to titillate your deep appetites.

Milk and Meat

"That the combining of meat and milk for the preparation of a food is reckoned to be so farfetched and so vile is evidenced by the fact that man is forbidden to benefit therefrom, to cook them together and to eat therefrom.

In order to emphasize the wrong involved in robbing the kid of its rightful sanctuary, the milk-filled udders of its mother, and in order that man should realize in due course that the living was never intended to end up in man's ever-craving stomach, this law forbidding (in all its severity) the combining of milk and meat was formulated.

Its purpose is to act as an ethical reminder during the period of transition (i.e. until the happy days when divine logic will prevail) that the taking of milk is equivalent to the taking of meat, as it is obtained in a manner that causes suffering and loss to living creatures...."

That Which Is Torn (Treifah)

The prohibition to eat the carcases of animals found in the fields and that of animals which have fallen prey to wild animals, highlights the feeling of righteous compassion that emanates from the pure heart of man.

It emphasizes the necessity of bringing assistance to animals in case of need.

Man must not link himself to the class of predatory animals by consuming that which has been killed and torn in the fields, for in so doing they share their booty and act in accordance with their way of life (of the predatory animals).

The fact that there is no difference [according to kashruth] between an animal who has died of sickness and one who has been torn by wild animals expresses in more than any other way the meaning of the feeling of compassion, in that *one must not benefit from the suffering of animals irrespective of the cause,* i.e. sickness or cruelty....

Those who participated in the compilation and the setting down of the basic concepts of the Religious Vegetarians have wittingly or unwittingly drawn up a spiritual blueprint for tomorrow's world, a world that will only be able to continue its existence and progress if the life and conduct of humanity be permeated with the spirit of divine compassion, a compassion that embraces both the human and the animal world....

Yet the answers that men seek to the problems of today and tomorrow lie hidden in the depths of the Torah (Bible); thus the loyalty of the masses is an intuitive one. They cling to the Bible because something within them tells them that somewhere within its circumference are lights that will illuminate their way, not only across the bridge of transition, but also to the world of tomorrow.

The Religious Vegetarians have shown the way. They have done more than that; they have presented the method, the key that will open many a seemingly locked door.

Let us follow in their footsteps and endeavor to obtain from within the depths of the Torah an answer and a guide to the problems that face us and the world.

There can be no turning back. It can be done and it will be done.

It is an historic imperative.

Eating Meat May Be Contrary To Judaism

Rabbi David Brusin

Parashat Beha'alotecha (this week's Torah portion of the Week) is not easy to read, as I will try to explain.

It poses a challenge to a part of our everyday lives that we would prefer to leave undisturbed--namely, the food we eat. Yet this should not surprise us. Judaism is relevant precisely because it addresses the ordinary, the commonplace in our lives.

The Torah does not hesitate to list foods that are permitted and prohibited, though it offers no overall explanation or rationale for the placement of foods on one side or the other. What we know of biblical eating habits revolves around the fact that "meat is never included among the staple diet of the children of Israel." Their diet is confined to agricultural products.

The concept of Israel as a "land flowing with milk and honey" plainly does not include an image of large, well organized and operated cattle ranches or chicken farms. One wonders, consequently, whether vegetarianism is a legitimate and nobler expression of Kashrut, the system of dietary laws formulated and developed through rabbinic interpretation of biblical texts and precedents.

Following instructions regarding the portable Tabernacle, central to the Israelites' desert period, we read in Beha'alotecha of a potential insurrection. The people are, understandably, worried about their future, nostalgic about their past (yes, in Egypt), and definitely sick and tired of being on the road and being homeless. This growing unrest and uncertainty leads to a forceful protest having to do with the Israelites' diet the past year.

Plague kills meat eaters

In an emotionally charged encounter with Moses, the Israelites cry out for what they think they need and want: "If only we had meat to eat." (Numbers 11:4).

It is not always possible to articulate or respond appropriately to a present source of pain and anxiety. The Israelites have misperceived theirs.

Soon after eating meat, a plague kills the offenders (Numbers 11:33). Fittingly, the place is named *kivrot hataavah,* the graves of craving; "because the people who had the craving were buried there" (11:34).

There is considerable reason to view this incident as a challenge to our own eating habits, regardless of whether we take Kashrut seriously. There is a growing body of evidence linking cancer of the colon, heart disease, high blood pressure and stroke to meat consumption.

Furthermore, there is the modern phenomenon of "factory farming," the morally repugnant system of raising animals in crowded stalls or cubicles, tethered at the neck and unable to move. The life cycle of such animals is determined solely on the basis of productivity and profits.

The morally sensitive concept of *shechitah* (humane, ritual slaughtering), an essential aspect of rabbinic Kashrut, is being undermined by such farming techniques.

Obviously, we would rather not be reminded of such facts. Yet our failure to act may involve irrevocable consequences for our children as well as for ourselves.

Beha'alotecha constitutes a warning. We are being warned that a "craving for meat" may be antithetical to what Judaism and Kashrut represent. We are being challenged to rethink what we now label kosher, Jewishly fit and proper for human beings to eat, given current methods of meat and poultry production.

Our physical well-being and our moral sensibilities hang in the balance.

Vegetarianism: The Ideal Of The Bible
Rabbi Sidney Clayman

If you seek Biblical support for vegetarian principles you have not far to go. There could not be a clearer mandate than in the first chapter of the first book of the Bible where the first dietary law was laid down. "And God said, 'Behold I have given unto you every herb yielding seed which is upon the face of the earth, and every tree in which is the fruit of the tree yielding seed; unto you it shall be for food.'"

Many Jewish commentators remark that according to the terms of this passage no animal, fowl or fish was permitted for food. Certainly the diet prescribed in this verse is vegetarian. It is explicitly and unequivocally stated.

But what became of this original dietary law? Alas, it must have been completely ignored very soon. By the time we reach the age of Noah, people not only ate meat, but also showed a callous disregard for the suffering of living creatures. A new law was therefore promulgated which, while permitting meat, forbade the cruel habit of tearing limbs from living creatures. This law was called אבר סן קהי ׳ and was part of Noah's code of Seven Basic Laws, laying down the absolute minimum standard of civilized conduct.

This second dietary law of Noah's code is distinctly inferior in tone, a far cry from the original. We can deduce from it how depraved people had become in the course of ten generations from Adam to Noah. No wonder the Bible tells us that "The imagination of the heart of man is wicked." But what was to become of the original and vegetarian diet?

It was not abandoned. Another attempt was made many years later. When the Israelites were in the wilderness, a vegetarian diet was tried out in the form of "Manna." According to the Rabbis, it had whatever taste and flavor the eater wished. This was indeed a miracle, but I suspect that it had not so much every taste as nutrient value, because God said, "It is the diet I have given unto you for food." It could not have formed the Israelites' main source of food unless it contained ample food content.

And it is interesting to note the phrase, "I have given unto you for food." This is reminiscent of the words, "Unto you it shall be for food" in the first chapter of the Bible, suggesting a link with it.

The second vegetarian attempt to introduce a vegetarian diet met with the same disappointing response as the first one. Expressions such as "We are sick of this light accursed food" or "We want meat," indicate utter and complete rejection. Moses was even in danger of losing his life for all his pains. The strong reaction was not because the Manna was inadequate but because of the Evil Inclination.*

(The serpents which bit, burned and poisoned the people, as read in the Biblical account, were nothing more than the Evil Inclination. When the Israelites looked up at the bronze serpent set up on a high pole, they saw a representation of the serpent-like Inclination within their own hearts, which had prompted this rebellious conduct.)

We are not entitled to censure and much less to condemn the Israelites in the wilderness. Very few of us would react differently in similar circumstances. When I was in a Vegetarian Guest House a few years ago, one of the guests confided in me that as soon as he got home he would get his teeth into a good, solid steak. His remarks reminded me of the cry of the Israelites over three and a half thousand years ago. "We want meat." The overwhelming majority of people would react in exactly the same way even today.

(But why was the 'Manna' experiment made? Did not God the Omniscient know the results in advance? It is reasonable for the believer in the Torah to infer that God wishes us to know that He intended a meatless diet and these intentions were frustrated by the power of the Evil Inclination.)

After this second failure, the next step was to regulate

meat foods by means of the Jewish dietary laws which are still in practice up to this day. Meat is not forbidden but the right is limited and there are many rules to be observed, too many to be discussed in this article.

Many explanations have been suggested as to the reasons for the restrictions of the Jewish dietary laws and the principles which govern them. The best comment which I know is in the Midrash: "The commandments were given in order to refine human nature."

How necessary this exercise is can be judged from the reaction to the first dietary laws in the Bible, and from the reaction of the Israelites in the wilderness to the Manna.

In our own time during the war against the Nazis, many Jews who were evacuated to towns and villages where Kosher meat was not available ate Treifah rather than adapt themselves to a meatless diet. The appetite is the most powerful instinct in human beings.

I should not like to venture my own comments on our dietary code.

The words THIS and THESE are very prominent in the Biblical text of our dietary laws. THIS kind of animal you may eat; THIS kind of fish you may eat; THESE kind of fowl you may not eat. The effect of the two words is, as our Rabbis agree, to exclude. They exclude all other types or species. A line is drawn across all flesh foods, animals, fish, fowl and all living creatures, as if to convey God's command--so far and no further. The eating of meat in the Jewish dietary laws is not the ultimate goal but a concession only to human weakness. THIS and THESE in the context warn us, "Don't abuse the concession by trespassing beyond the border line."

When a Jew breaks the dietary laws and eats forbidden flesh he often excuses himself by asking what wrong he is doing. The wrong he is doing is to break the barrier of our Torah and he is leading himself and others towards a world of uncontrolled appetite with the Evil Inclination unrestrained.

But what becomes now of the first dietary law in the first chapter of the first book of the Bible? Is it replaced and abandoned forever? It could not have been meant for the use of the earliest generations only, for so very short a time, and from then onwards to be ignored forever more. If that were the case there would be no point in recording the passage at all.

The passage still stands in our Bible, supreme. It seems to say to us, "This is the High Ideal of God, and all other standards are but stages towards it." It is there for us and for the whole world to see the ultimate goal for which all good men and women should strive.

* Ed. note: Traditional Judaism believes that human behavior is controlled by a "Good Inclination" and an "Evil Inclination," but that human beings can control "the Evil Inclination."

Enhancing The Divine Image

Rabbi Stephen Fuchs

For the past seven years I have been a vegetarian. I do not eat meat, fish or chicken. I do, however, use eggs and dairy products.* The criterion for what I eat is simple. I eat nothing that has to die for me to consume it.

The foundation of the vegetarian life-style I have adopted is not medical. Neither does it come from a distaste for the taste of flesh. I am one who loved a good steak or a good hamburger or a piece of roast beef. The memories of our chicken dinners on Friday night or the duck or goose we consumed on special occasions are precious to me. No, my decision to become a vegetarian is not based on a distaste for meat. Quite the contrary.

My decision to become a vegetarian is based on my understanding of the essential message of the early chapters of Genesis. First and foremost is the story of creation. Much has been written about this story over the years. Most people think of it as either the scientific account of how the world was created or a fairy tale which offers little meaningful guidance to us today. From my perspective, both of these interpretations are wrong. In his book, *In the Beginning,* the late science fiction writer Isaac Asimov fell into the trap of viewing the creation story as an obsolete scientific document when he wrote, "The biblical writers did the best they could with the scientific material available to them. If they had written those earlier chapters of Genesis knowing what we know today, we can be certain they would have written it completely differently."[1] No, Mr. Asimov, we cannot be so certain. The biblical authors were not concerned with making a scientific statement any more than Mozart was concerned with writing "Rock 'N Roll" music. The biblical authors were concerned with making a religious statement, and the statement they made continues to inspire people today.

So, the first component of my decision to become vegetarian deals with an interpretation of the creation story. No, it is not bad science. It is simply not science at all. The creation story is, though, an exquisite religious poem, and it has a powerful message for us. The basis of the story is the notion that the creation of the world was a purposeful act--not an accident. In the assertion that creation was purposeful, the creation account in the Torah stands apart from other religious creation stories which see the world as we know it as an incidental by-product of interactions among gods with human qualities such as fear, jealousy and sexuality.[2]

God's purposefulness and intentionality also separate the Genesis account from scientific theories which assume that the world in which we live began as the result of an accident of nature. The Torah's creation story assumes that behind creation is a Creator who set the process in motion. The orderliness and purposefulness of the creation account are apparent from the economy of language, the repetition of certain key phrases and, most significantly, from the way that each succeeding action of creation bases itself on that which precedes it.

Clearly, it is the intent of the biblical author to proclaim humanity as God's highest creative act. Light, land, vegetation, fish, fowl and beasts of the earth were all, the creation poem asserts, created by *fiat*---by the simple proclamation "And God said, 'Let there be...' and it was so."

Only in the case of humanity does God ponder the task of creation. Only humanity is given "dominion over the fish of the sea, the birds of the sky, the cattle, the whole earth and all the creeping things that creep on earth (Genesis 1:26). Only in the case of humanity does God depart from the "Let there be...and it was so" formula. We human beings alone, the Bible asserts, were created in God's image. Jewish tradition makes clear that God has no form or shape, so that "created in God's image" cannot mean that we look like God. Rather, the expression means that we alone among the acts of creation share some of God's characteristics. "Created in God's image" means that we, more than any other creatures, are responsible for the quality of life on earth.

It is ours to replenish or ruin, to protect or to pollute. That indeed is the ultimate purpose of the story: to remind us that we are in charge. We should not glory in our power, but realize our responsibilities as stewards of creation. To "have dominion" over the fish of the sea, the birds of the air, and the beasts of the earth, does not mean to exploit them mercilessly. For me it means "to be responsible for," to understand that we are the most powerful creatures on earth, and that we can rule with either kindness or cruelty. Kindness toward living creatures is part of my understanding of the message of the creation story.

Among the many rabbinic comments on the opening chapter of Genesis is the one which notes that the word "creation" (*Bereshit,* the first word of the Bible) begins with the letter *beth* because *beth* is the first letter of the word *bracha,* which means "blessing." Creation begins with *beth* to remind us that each person has the potential by her or his actions to make life a blessing for ourselves, for those around us, for the other creatures God created and for future generations.[3]

Chapters two through eleven in Genesis, the chapters which follow the story of creation, tell, as I interpret them, of three attempts on God's part to create what has been from the beginning God's highest goal: a caring, compassionate society. Each of those societies has groundrules.[4] Essentially, though, the first society in Eden was a place of no birth, no death, no sexuality (in my view) and no need to work hard. It was a place in which human beings were given to eat of vegetation only. The second society is one which I label "Post-Eden/Pre-Flood." That society was a place of birth, death, sexuality and the need to work for a living. It didn't work out any better than the other two. The Torah pictures the Almighty as constantly trying to make adjustments, even compromises, with human nature, so that society might work out better.

After the flood, there are new ground rules. First, God promises never to destroy the world again (Genesis 8:22). Second, people are to be responsible for their actions (Genesis 9:6). Third and most important for our discussion, for the first time, after the flood, humanity received permission to eat meat (Genesis 9:3). All of the foregoing, though, shows us that in the first two attempts God made to set up a workable society, human beings were vegetarian. Perhaps it was as a concession to human nature that we are given permission to eat meat in a third attempt to set up a society that would be workable. As we know, that third society didn't work out either, and God made a fourth attempt to set up a caring, compassionate society through the covenant which the Almighty made with Abraham and Sarah. The permission that we received to eat meat is still in force, of course, and subsequent Jewish tradition has curtailed that privilege by reminding us through elaborate rituals of *kashrut* of the magnitude of what we do each time we kill a living being.

I have not been able, though, to shake the notion that if we really wanted to do God's will, we would abstain from meat altogether. In short, I believe I more fully approach my potential as a creature created in God's image when I abstain from eating food that must die so that I might eat it. Though much has changed in the course of history and much has happened to our people, I still believe our purpose as Jews is to be exponents of God's hope to create the caring, compassionate society for which God has yearned since creation. For me, part of that quest has been to abstain from eating meat, not because I don't like it, not because I am worried by its effect on my health, but because I believe it helps me to achieve the divine potential with which God made me. I cannot claim that my analysis of the sources and the basis for my decision provide incontrovertible evidence that God wants us to be vegetarian. I only know that, for me, I feel better about myself and more wholehearted in my attempt to take my place as a covenantal partner with God in fulfilling the charge first made to Abram, "Be a blessing," the blessing God intended in using the letter *beth* to begin the story of creation.

Notes

1 Isaac Asimov, *In the Beginning* (New York: Crown Publishers, 1981), 3.

2 Edward Lavitt and Robert McDowell, *In the beginning...Creation Stories for Young People* (New York: The Third Press, 1973). The book contains 35 examples of creation stories from throughout the world which illustrate this point.

3 *Bereshit Raba* 1:10

4 For a fuller discussion of these ground rules, see my doctoral thesis, *Standing at Sinai: Looking Backward, Looking Forward* (Nashville, Tennessee: Vanderbilt University, 1992), 28-54.

* The following is a response from Rabbi Fuchs after the editor wrote a letter to him, pointing out that under contemporary farming conditions, eggs and dairy products are the products of the same inhumane conditions as meat itself:

"Thank you very much for your thoughtful response to the essay which I sent you. You have given me much to think about. In regard to the points in your last paragraph concerning eggs and dairy products, the information you sent is new to me. I must give this a lot of thought and, at some point, may indeed reformulate my approach to eggs and milk based on what you have said. You have allowed me to begin thinking in a new way. The point that I made was that an animal does not have to die for us to use its eggs or its milk. I wonder whether there are farms today where animals are raised humanely and compassionately..."

The Universal Chorus

Rabbi Everett Gendler

In recent decades many authors have presented many good reasons for adopting and following a vegetarian diet. Some of the reasons concern health: we'll be healthier if we avoid eating animal flesh and its derivatives. Other reasons stem from other ethical considerations: to reduce the total suffering on our planet by reducing the suffering of animals; to increase the availability of food for all humans by eating lower on the food chain; to help to assure the future of the earth by consuming fewer resources to sustain ourselves. These are compelling considerations, and they have persuaded many to adopt such a diet.

There is an additional consideration that I'd like to share, this one deriving from one possible answer to the basic question of our ultimate purpose in this life on this planet. Let me state very simply this sense of purpose, support it with some traditional Jewish sources, and suggest how a vegetarian diet makes it possible for us to fulfill this purpose with greater ease and enthusiasm.

Why are we here? To exult in Creation! To sing God's praises! To enjoy the gifts of our life here on earth with full awareness, and to give voice to this enjoyment with words of poetry, songs of praise, and sounds of joyous appreciation.

On first reading, this may seem a bit odd. Is God, then, the Cosmic Music Lover par excellence? Before dismissing such a notion, consider how ancient and basic to human expression are rhythm and melody. If our creation in the Divine image means that there are at least some significant resemblances between the Divine and the human, then such a notion is, upon reflection, not at all far fetched.

Eric Gill, a visionary modern craftsman, communitarian, and creative Catholic thinker whose outlook was profoundly influenced by the Hebrew as well as the Christian Bible, put it vividly and even more radically:

> "The Lord is a singer; the work of creation is a song--the morning stars sang together.
> And in a song all things must sing...
> (God) is a singer. The created universe is a little song of his---a little song, but big enough and loud enough for us---we are notes in it. There is no other explanation of the universe or of us."

Gill's daring formulation strikes me as a wonderful summary-in-image of what many a verse from Psalms proclaims. To cite just a few verses from four psalms which are part of every Sabbath morning service (and three of the four are recited also in the daily morning service):

> Rejoice in the Lord, O you righteous,
> Praise befits the upright.
> Praise the Lord with the lyre;
> make melody to him with the harp of ten strings.
> Sing to him a new song;
> play skillfully amid shouts of joy (33:1-3)

> Sing to the Lord with thanksgiving;
> make melody to our God on the lyre. (147:7)

> Praise the Lord!
> How good it is to sing praises to our God...
> Sing to the Lord with thanksgiving;
> make melody to our God on the lyre. (149:1,7)

> Praise God with trumpet sound,
> praise him with lute and harp!
> Praise him with tambourine and dance;
> praise him with strings and pipe!
> Praise him with clanging cymbals;
> praise him with loud clashing cymbals (150:3-5)

Especially pertinent to this essay, however, is one additional psalm that is also part of every traditional morning service, weekdays, Sabbaths, and Festivals. Psalm 148 begins:

> Praise the Lord!
> Praise the Lord from the heavens;
> Praise the Lord in the heights!

Sun, moon, and stars of light are summoned to praise the Divine along with angels and hosts of heaven. It continues:

> Praise the Lord from the earth

and summon to the praise of God sea monsters and all deeps, fire and hail, snow and frost, vapor and stormy wind, mountains and hills, fruit trees and cedars, beasts and cattle, creeping things and winged fowl, along with women and men both young and old, and persons from all stations of life. (See Psalm 148). Clearly we are not the only singers in this chorus of praise to the Creator, but are to join in a universal chorus of praise whose members include all of creation, including all our fellow creatures with whom we share this earth: beasts and cattle, creeping things and winged fowl.

This tradition is not confined to the Psalms, nor does it end with the Bible. The Song of the Three Jews, found in the Apocrypha as an addition to the Book of Daniel, and probably a Hebrew composition, also summons all the works of the Lord to sing God's praise with exaltation.

> Bless the Lord, all you works of the Lord,
> Sing God's praise and exalt God forever...
> Bless the Lord...whales and all that
> swim in the waters...
> all birds of the air...all beasts and cattle...
> all people on earth...

Once again we find our fellow animals included with us in this summons to praise the Source of all Creation.

Even more striking is the portrayal of all living creatures singing their individual songs in praise of the Creator. In Perek Shira, A Chapter of Song, a mystical hymn (dating from the 5th-7th century) that even today is found in all complete traditional Hebrew prayer books, worded songs are ascribed specifically to land animals, winged creatures, insects, and residents of the waters. Cows, camels, horses, mules; roosters, chickens, doves, eagles; butterflies, locusts, spiders, flies; sea monsters, fish, frogs: all of these and many more offer Biblical words of praise in song to their Creator, filling the universe with hymns and songs.

If, indeed, our purpose is to join with all of sentient creation in songs of praise to the Creator; if, in fact, the universe resounds with sounds of singing from all its living creatures; if, in truth, we are members of a chorus, not isolated soloists, then harmony among the choristers is evidently desirable. The better the terms of our relations with our fellow chorus members, the more natural the singing and the more beautiful the blending of voices and sounds. To respect the life of our fellow choir members by not killing them and eating their corpses would seem an obviously desirable condition for choral collegiality. To see other animals as fellow celebrants of life rather than primarily as potential corpses awaiting our consumption would surely affect not only their singing, but ours as well.

To say this is not to sentimentalize our relations with other animals. Messianic visions of the peaceable kingdom are precisely that, Messianic visions whose fulfillment awaits a radical transformation of life conditions on this earth. Until that time (or end of time), rivalries and competition between humans and other species seem destined to persist. Yet to recognize that we inhabit a planet where much of life is companionable as well as competitive, and could become more companionable, would surely have significant effects on how we feel and how we live. Indeed, to apply the famous verse of Psalm 137 to this rather different context:

> How shall we sing the Lord's song
> in a foreign land? (137:4)

in a land where we feel isolated and alien from the creatures who surround us? To discover (or perhaps recover) some sense of kinship with our fellow creatures might, over time, have effects on our lives quite beyond our imagining in the mere articulation of this notion.

But is this idea of singing our way through life with life really Jewish, one might ask? By way of a suggestive supplement to the verses earlier cited, let me conclude by transmitting a verse from Talmud that I learned from that remarkable and inspired ethicist, mystic, and music lover, the late Rabbi Abraham Joshua Heschel, whose memory is truly a blessing:

> Rabbi Akiba said:
> A song every day!
> Chant every day!
>
> ---Sanhedrin 99b

May that become our philosophy and our practice as well.

Full Moon of Tammuz 5755
12 July 1995

Seek My Face, Speak My Name

Rabbi Arthur Green

"To Work It And Guard It": Preserving God's World

...As we seek to articulate a Judaism appropriate to a new era of Jewish history, we cannot fail to note that this period begins in the same decades when the human race realizes it has achieved the gruesome possibility of destroying the planet on which we all live. The rabbis tell us that shortly after Adam was created, God walked him around the Garden of Eden and told him to take care to guard the world that he was being given. "If you destroy this world," he was told, "there is no one to come and set it right after you." Such an *aggadah* has a level of intense meaning in our age that the early rabbis could hardly have foretold.

Telling the tale of Creation is itself a statement of love of the natural world. It needs to be accompanied by actions that bear witness to that love--without these it is false testimony. The ethic that proceeds from this tale is one of strong commitment to *ahavat ha-bri-ot,* the love of all God's creatures, and a sense of absolute responsibility for their survival. (For us Jews, after all, love and responsibility always go hand in hand!) This is a world view in which the love of God and love for the world, including both the natural and the human dimensions, are in no way separable from one another. A piety that proclaims the love of God, without showing it by a love for world, is theologically self-contradictory. It is the natural world that embodies the only God we know. The tale of Creation achieves its fulfillment in acts we undertake to make our appreciation of divinity real by the way we live. We do so both in our individual personal lives and in the commitments we make to greater causes. The needs of the world are so great and so urgent that they cannot be adequately addressed only by a life of personal purification that creates a "holy" elite, but does nothing more to help the world survive.

Here, too, the details are hard to specify, and each person and community has to find ways to fulfill these commandments. By way of example, it surely seems right that we achieve a high level of consciousness and action regarding the ways we live, the products we use, and the ways we dispose of them. We must stop being callous and excessive users of earth's resources. We must become aware and share with others the realization that a small minority of the human race consumes far more than its appropriate share of earth's resources. We need to concern ourselves with the continued availability for generations to come of pure air, pure water, and good earth that will yield untainted produce. As good Jewish parents, concerned always with providing for our children, we must not allow ourselves to consume the legacy that belongs to future generations. The many areas in which to become active in ways helpful to the world's survival hardly need enumerating here. Each of us must find significant means to become partners in giving attention to such concerns. The fact that we band together in such activities with persons of good will who relate to the divine through other traditions (or without the language of traditional religion), is all for the good. There is an authentic *kiddush ha-Shem* in expressions of our Jewish faith that can be shared in such a way with others. The example of Abraham and Sarah, who fulfilled their love of God by making God beloved to others, is the starting point of our renewal of the Jewish moral life. The open tent of our first parents, into which all were welcomed and where all were fed and taught by example, must once again be open to others in our old-new home.

Another series of *mitsvot* that proceeds directly from a relationship with this Creation tale is that which is called in Hebrew by the general term *tsa'ar ba'aley hayyim* ("the suffering of living beings") or sympathy with pain caused to animals. Our story of Creation tells us that we humans were created on the same day as were the land animals. Here again, even with the Genesis tale, we are being told that we are less separable from the animal kingdom than other aspects of that story may lead us to think. The Creation tale also makes us rulers over the animal kingdom, but only as God's viceroy who bears responsibility to the ultimate Ruler. This role demands of us that we be sympathetic to the suffering of other creatures, and we not cause them needless pain. A commitment to preserving the earth also means a commitment to preserving the great and wondrous variety of life species in which the One is manifest.

Vegetarianism: A Kashrut For Our Age

In this spirit, I believe the time has come for us to reconsider the question of whether we should continue to consume animal flesh as food. Our tradition has always contained within it a certain provegetarian bias, even though it has provided for the eating of meat. In the ideal state of Eden, according to the Bible, humans ate only plants; we and the animals together were given the plants as food. Only after the expulsion from Eden, when the urge overwhelmed humans and led them toward evil, did the consumption of flesh begin. The very first set of laws given to humanity sought to limit this evil by forbidding the flesh of a still-living creature, placing a limit on acts of cruelty or terror related to the eating of animal flesh. The Torah's original insistence that domestic animals could be slaughtered only for purpose of sacrifice, an offering to God needed to atone for the killing, was compromised only when the Book of Deuteronomy wanted to insist that sacrifice be offered in Jerusalem alone. Realizing that people living at a great distance could not bring all their animals to the Temple for slaughter, the "secular" slaughter and eating of domesticated animals was permitted. Even then, the taboo against consuming blood, and later, the requirement to salt meat until even traces of blood were removed, "for the blood is the self" of the creature, represent a clear discomfort with the eating of animal flesh. Most significantly, the forbidding of any mixing of milk and meat represents a proto-vegetarian sensibility. Milk is the fluid by which life is passed on from generation to generation; it may not be consumed with flesh, representing the taking of that life in an act of violence. The fluid of life may not be mixed with that of death. As the Torah says of the hewn-stone altar: "For you have waved your sword over it and have profaned it."

The reasons for acting upon this vegetarian impulse in our day are multiple and compelling, *just as compelling, I believe, as the reasons for the selective taboos against certain animals must have been when the Community of Israel came to accept these as the word of God.* This is what we mean, after all, when we talk about a *mitsvah* being "the word of God" or "God's will." It is a form of human expression or a way of acting that feels compellingly right. This rightness has both a moral and a spiritual dimension; it is an expression of values we choose, but it also makes a more profound statement about who we are. We then come to associate it with divinity, and it becomes a vehicle through which we express our spiritual selves. With the passage of time, origins are shrouded in mystery, and the form becomes the "will of God." Israelites of ancient times felt that way about the taboos widely current in their society against the consumption of certain animals that they saw as repulsive, against the eating of blood, the mixing of milk and meat, and so forth. They associated this series of taboos with the God of Sinai. Over the centuries, *kashrut* as we know it became a *mitsvah*, a way in which Jews are joined to God.

Our situation has certain important parallels to this one. We are urgently concerned with finding a better way to share earth's limited resources. We know that many more human lives can be sustained if land is used for planting rather than for grazing of animals for food. We are committed also to a healthier way of living and are coming to recognize that the human is, after all, a mostly vegetarian species. But for us as Jews, the impulse is largely a moral and religious one. We have a long tradition of abhorring violence. Cruelty to animals has long been forbidden by Jewish law and sensibilities. Our tradition tells us that we must shoo a mother bird away from the nest before we take her eggs so that she does not suffer as we break the bond between them. We are told that a mother and her calf may not be slaughtered on the same day. The very next step beyond these prohibitions is a commitment to a vegetarian way of living.

We Jews in this century have been victims of destruction and mass slaughter on an unprecedented scale. We have seen every norm of humanity violated as we were treated like cattle rather than human beings. Our response to this memory is surely a complex and multitextured one. But as we overcome the understandable first reactions to the events, some of us feel our abhorrence of violence and bloodshed growing so strong that it reaches even beyond the borders of the human and into the animal kingdom. We Jews, who always looked upon killing for sport or pleasure as something alien and repulsive, should now, out of our own experience, be reaching the point where we find even the slaughter of animals for food morally beyond the range of the acceptable. If Jews have to be associated with killing at all in our time, let it be only for the defense of human life. Life has become too precious in this era for us to be involved in the shedding of blood, even that of animals, when we can survive without it. This is not an ascetic choice, we should note, but rather a life-affirming one. A vegetarian Judaism would be more whole in its ability to embrace the presence of God in all of Creation.

To Your Health

Rabbi Sidney J. Jacobs

Good health isn't a matter of luck. You do have control over your body. By making the proper choices, you can trade in a sluggish body that causes pain and makes you irritable for a vigorous one that allows you to enjoy every moment more.

The fundamental ingredient to achieving radiant health is the food we eat.

Selecting that food is no longer a mystery. Your basic shopping list has been prepared for you and presented to you in the Hebrew Bible! There, in the Book of *Genesis*, God said, "See, I give you every seed-bearing plant that is upon the earth, and every tree that has seed-bearing fruit: they shall be yours for food....of every tree of the garden, you may freely eat...and you shall eat the grains of the field." (1:29, 2:16, 3:18)

That this plant-based diet should be featured in *Genesis* is really amazing. It is the diet that progressive epidemiologists, nutritionists and physicians are recommending for health and longevity as we approach the 21st century. The grain-centered, fiber-rich diet, which epidemiological and clinical studies have indicated reduces the risks of heart disease, hypertension, most cancer, multiple sclerosis, tumors, kidney disease, osteoporosis, diabetes, arthritis, and other degenerative diseases, is thousands of years old.

This is the high-fiber, low-fat diet that contains all of the protein, calcium and other minerals and vitamins needed not only to sustain life, but also to prevent the ghastly diseases unique to a society that gorges on animal foods, white flour products and refined sugar.

Many vegetarian nutritionists recommend taking a Vitamin B-12 supplement.

This is the health-maintaining, vegetarian diet that not only can keep us safe from treacherous degenerative diseases but can also protect us from minor but annoying health problems that gnaw away at our moods and productivity, problems such as overweight, impotence, dental caries, stomach aches, headaches, colds, sore throats and irritability.

It is also the violence-free diet that reduces animal suffering and can help ameliorate world hunger. The ecologically sound diet that makes for a healthier us also makes for a healthier planet.

Cuisine free of animal products is not only nutritious but delicious and money-saving.

Everyone at the table had three servings of everything the night we brought out heaping dishes of buckwheat and whole wheat pasta tossed with extra virgin olive oil, chopped vine-ripened tomatoes, fresh basil, crushed garlic and sliced mushroom; carrots and cabbage slaw and tofu banana pie--mashed tofu mixed with mashed bananas, doused with cherry cider and spiked with pure vanilla.

A Sunday night dinner at our home, shared with good friends, led off with crisp crudites--carrots, celery, zucchini, mushrooms, cherry tomatoes, green onions and broccoli--heaped on a 20-inch stoneware plate. A tangy, tofu dill sauce was there for the dipping. Steaming bowls of zesty lentil chili followed, together with sides of golden brown rice. Slices of apple baked with vanilla and cinnamon and a few squirts of pure apple juice on a bed of rolled oats was served for dessert. The meal was tasteful, peaceful and warming.

Many people who have switched to this complex carbohydrate diet wonder why they didn't get into it long ago. Once you delight in the scrumptious fare, you'll love it.

Try barley soup, brown rice and a wok of vegetables, grain burgers, whole grain pasta, millet and vegetable casseroles, bean soups and stews, stuffed baked potatoes, pita bread pocket sandwiches, nuts and seeds (some people soak them for easier digestion), baskets of oven "fried" potatoes (sliced thin and baked to a crispy texture), rice cakes with peanut butter, cut up veggies and whole grain toast sliced into squares. Tantalize your taste buds with ethnic treats such as tostadas, spaghetti, curry. Health food stores feature tofu hot dogs and a variety of burgers. Just remember to keep the vegetable fats such as nuts and oils to a minimum.

Scout your bookstore for vegetarian recipe books to help you make the transition....

So many people we know have become disenchanted with strict regimens in which you measure four ounces of this, slathered with a level, half-teaspoon of that, capped with two square inches of something else. We have watched good people torture themselves for days, weeks and, in some cases, for months, usually in a majestic effort to shed pounds.

With rare exceptions, even the most impressive weight losses are temporary, because no change in lifestyle occurs. On the other hand, a food style devoid of animal products allows the body to lose weight naturally and to keep that weight off. We wish you could meet every person we know who has made this change.

One day, while pouring millet into bags in a health food store on Beverly Boulevard in Los Angeles, we were interrupted by a sweet voice asking if we could reach up for a package of stoneground, whole wheat bagels. As we handed the bagels over, we were struck by the woman's complexion. She had skin as smooth as alabaster, etched with just a few wrinkles. Her blue eyes were clear. She wore no lipstick, and yet her lips were rich with color. Her white hair was thick and lustrous. Her posture was perfect, her voice vibrant. She had asked us to reach for the bagels only because we were blocking her path.

She was 93! For the past 50 years, she said, she had been eating a diet in which brown rice, whole wheat, barley, oatmeal and beans were her staples. She ate no animal products. She proudly told us that in all that time she had never been ill. She was happy and excited about life.

How many times have you heard that you are what you eat? Your food really does become part of you. A friend of ours reported that one day she gazed over her dinner plate of meat, greasy potatoes, white rolls and sugar-glazed carrots served up on fine china in a trendy restaurant. (This glop had a high price.) She imagined the contents of her plate flowing through her systems and decided right then and there to switch to what she calls her "grain and green" style of eating. Friends who haven't seen her in a while says she looks years younger. A colleague at work teases her that she's really the younger, peppier sister of her former self.

In *Deuteronomy 8:7-9,* it is written: "a land of wheat and barley and vines, and fig trees and pomegranates, a land of olive oil and honey; a land wherein you shall eat bread without scarceness, you shall not lack anything in it...."
Grains, vegetables and fruits--this is what we can assume God wanted for us.

In *Ezekiel 4:9,* we even find a recipe for bread: "...take wheat, barley, beans, lentils, millet and emmer (oats). Put them into one vessel and bake them into bread."

We have met many people who maintain that personal circumstances make it impossible for them to change their diet. A man we know who had heart disease says he attends many business lunches and dinners. People will think he's sick, he says, if he doesn't eat the customary rubber meat, white cotton rolls stripped of their fiber, the salty, soggy, buttered vegetables and the sugary, gooey desserts.

One woman claims that she entertains often, and that her guests expect platters of cheeses and sweets.

How many times have we heard the saga of the grandfather who lived to be 97? You know, the nonagenarian who throughout his life stuffed himself with meat, fried foods, candy and ice cream. He also pushed aside anything on his plate that was green or yellow and smoked a corn cob pipe. Grandpa might have lucked out. Will you? It's your choice.

Of course, change is frightening. An anthropologist we know said diet is so culturally ingrained that many people can more easily be convinced to switch their religious beliefs than to alter their diet drastically. On holidays, we can almost smell the meals of celebrations past. The aromas of dinners served on the Sabbaths and Passovers waft across the years, even across the decades. We associate foods with events, with times when we felt protected and comforted. When we understand this, it is easier to change.

You have a choice. You can choose the grain-centered diet of *Genesis* for yourself, for your guests, for your precious family. You can enjoy the bounty of good health.

Your children can be more alert in school and free from frequent colds and infections. They can have the spunk that ejects them from a place in front of the television set and excites them to play ball, ride bikes, skate, draw, paint, sculpt, read and do chores. They are too dear to become the receptacles and conduits for the crunchy-munchy-crackle menu of junk and slurpy, sugary liquid that TV hucksters pitch to them.

By the way, sugar suppresses the body's immune system for as long as 48 hours after you eat it. It can depress your mood, too. Try skipping it for a few weeks, and watch your attitude change.

You can encourage your synagogue to replace the sweet rolls and chocolate brownies at the *Oneg Shabbat* after the services with brown rice raisin pudding, oatmeal raisin cookies, carob brownies, fruit, nuts and popcorn.
You can offer your guests food that will build their health instead of food that will make them feel guilty.

Let's stop providing excuses for each other to indulge in harmful eating. Let's stop playing the food games. You know the ones: "I fixed this just for you." "One piece won't hurt anybody."

We have seen so much suffering in so many families, suffering which could have been avoided. We have paced a hospital corridor with a beautiful young widow-to-be whose husband was dying of cancer. Not long before, we had heard from him how his meat diet and cigarette smoking couldn't hurt him.

We have looked into the eyes of the teen-age boy whose father promised he would begin to lose weight as soon as he completed his next business deal. The fatal heart attack didn't wait.

We have steadied the quivering bodies of elderly parents in mourning their middle-aged daughter, a brilliant academician, dead of breast-cancer.

You can choose not to put your loved one through the ordeal of your illness and possible demise. We appeal to you. Care enough about yourself. Choose life!

Choose a return to the diet of *Genesis,* the diet of the ideal world. Be aware that, according to a number of Jewish scholars, including Rabbi Abraham Isaac ha-Kohen Kook (1865-1935), first Chief Rabbi of pre-state Israel, permission to eat meat was given only after the Flood, when God observed that human beings had become so corrupt that this concession was made.

There followed regulations over the eating of meat, which resulted in the Jewish dietary laws of *Kashruth.*

For our psychic as well as for our physical well-being, we must become aware of the realities of slaughter of animals for food. So-designated "humane slaughter"--kosher and otherwise-is by its very nature a contradiction in terms. And the horrible method of slaughter does not even take into account the cruelty the animals suffer en route to the abattoir. Nor does it take into account that calves are snatched from their mothers at birth, placed in stalls in which they cannot even turn around, that baby chicks are debeaked and squashed into battery cages in which they are so crowded that the birds can barely move.

Can we be happy as human beings when our dinner plates are filled with the remains of animals who have lived in agony and died in fear? Can we nibble away at their flesh, their eggs, the milk and cheese that comes from horrors they have endured, and find peace within ourselves and the universe?

Rabbi Kook insisted that peace on earth presupposes peace between people and animals.

His successor, the first Ashkenazi Chief Rabbi of the State of Israel, the late Rabbi Isaac Herzog (1888-1959), asserted that "Man's carnivorous nature is not taken for granted or praised in the fundamental teachings of Judaism. The rabbis of the Talmud told that men were vegetarians in earliest times, between Creation and the generation of Noah....

"Judaism as a religion offers the option of eating animal flesh, and most Jews do, but in our own century....a whole galaxy of central rabbinic and spiritual leaders....has been affirming vegetarianism as the ultimate meaning of Jewish moral teaching. They have been proclaiming the autonomy of all living creatures as the value which our religious tradition must now teach to all of its believers....

"Jews will move increasingly to vegetarianism out of their own deepening knowledge of what their tradition commands as they understand it in this age."

The list of noted Jewish vegetarians includes two Nobel laureates in literature, Isaac Bashevis Singer and the late S.Y. Agnon (1888-1970), as well as the literary legend, Franz Kafka (1883-1924).

As we increase our reverence for all life, we increase reverence for ourselves, also, the reverence that can motivate us to take care of our bodies.

Jewish vegetarians join their non-Jewish peers in believing that vegetarianism can help alleviate world hunger. The world's land resources should be used to provide grains, vegetables and fruits for all instead of being ravaged to raise grain which is fed to animals who, in turn, are slaughtered to feed meat-eating human beings.

While the affluent consume animal products at breakfast, lunch and dinner, millions of the world's people starve. This is really ludicrous, when you consider that more than 80 percent of the corn and oats we grow is used to feed livestock, not people. More than half of the harvested farmland in the United States is used to grow food for livestock. One acre of land used to produce cattle feed will end up delivering 165 pounds of beef. That same acre could produce 20,000 pounds of potatoes, according to the Department of Agriculture. Our precious water resources, too, are evaporating, as half of the water we use in this country is used to irrigate land devoted to growing fodder for livestock.

To quench the appetite for meat, we have not only raped our own farmlands but have stripped the tropical rain forests of Central America and South America to convert them to pasture land for cattle.

We have the option of participating in the cruel and selfish system of animal food production or of cleansing ourselves of it.

In the Apocrypha (30:16), Ben Sira said, "There is no wealth like health."....You are a valuable human being who deserves care and nurturing. There is only one you. Sanctify your uniqueness. Remember, you can choose health. You can choose to eat the vegetarian, grain-based diet recommended in Genesis. You can choose to exercise. You can choose to limit your alcohol consumption. You can choose to stub out your cigarette habit and not to pop pills.

You can look at yourself and decide that you deserve to have only good things enter your body and good things happen to your body. The more you take care of yourself, the better you'll feel, and the more you'll like yourself. The more you like yourself, the better care you'll take.

"...and if not now, when?" You can choose life. Please do!

Vegetarianism

Rabbi Bonnie Koppell

The purpose and goal of Jewish living is to raise our consciousness of the presence of God in our every-day lives. Judaism, with its system of brakhot (blessings) for every experience from going to the bathroom to seeing a rainbow, teaches us that we do not need to remove ourselves from our daily routine in order to engender a sense of holiness. Rather, our challenge is to live with the chaos and tension of life in the modern world and, at the same time, to live lives of kedusha (holiness).

With the possible exception of sex, there is no more basic human activity than eating, rendering it an appropriate candidate for Jewish rituals designed to maintain our focus on Godliness. The table is seen as an altar, and the concern with Kashrut extends to removing knives, instruments of war, from the table during the Birkat HaMazon (blessing after the meal). Tsaar baalei khayim, the concern for the pain of all living things and the reverence for life, is another essential aspect of kashrut.

Vegetarianism is clearly the Torah's ideal; the Garden of Eden is a vegetarian society. Only after the generation of the flood, when God becomes reconciled to the inevitability of human evil, does meat-eating enter history. Kashrut, then, is a concession, an attempt to exercise control over the unrestrained consumption of meat. Even so, it is frowned upon in later tradition, as we read in the Talmud, "One should eat meat only if one has a special craving for it, and even then occasionally and sparingly." (Hullin 84a)

Today our concern for kashrut extends beyond issues of kosher slaughter, to examining the ways in which our food is grown and animals are raised. Rabbi Zalman Schachter questions the kashrut, for example, of eggs raised in "the concentration camp conditions of contemporary poultry ranches," "the kashrut of chemical additives, of cigarettes, or coal from strip mines." (*The First Step,* p. 75) Writing in *Tikkun* magazine, he adds to this list: "Is electricity from a nuclear reactor kosher? Or, is something bottled in a one-way bottle more or less kosher than something bottled in a recycled one?" These issues are being addressed by today's movement towards Eco-Kashrut, a kashrut standard that incorporates and then transcends the bounds of traditional practice.

As our planet shrinks, as our resources diminish, it behooves us to examine the inherent wastefulness and inequity in eating meat, when 90% of the protein directly available in the grains fed to livestock are wasted in the process. It has been estimated that 20 vegetarians could be fed using the same amount of land it takes to feed one meat eater. Consider the fact that it takes 25 gallons of water to produce one pound of wheat, and 2500 gallons to produce 1 pound of meat.[1] Why not just eat the food directly, prepared with love and with the requisite brakhot that raise our eating to the level of a religious experience?

As a rabbi I am often called upon to determine the kashrut of various food products and institutions. I am appalled by the number of chemicals that are added to our food, and long for the days when one did not need a degree in chemistry in order to understand what one was eating. From my perspective, I'm tempted to brand all food additives as treif, and hail as glatt kosher only those fruits and vegetables that are organically grown.

Judaism concedes our desire to eat animal flesh, and so we withdraw from the vegetarian ideal to the highly regulated system of kashrut. Rabbi Sheila Weinberg, writing in *The Jewish Family Book,* suggests that perhaps "a slice of meat, now and again, slaughtered and prepared according to those ancient laws, may guard us from this enticing delusion (that we have been redeemed)." I am attracted to her position, even as I acknowledge that we have all too many reminders in our world that we have not reached the Messianic age. Vegetarianism is an ideal way to actualize the Torah's vision of a world in which the divine spark in all creation is respected and revered.

[1] Robbins, John, *Diet for a New America*, NH: Stillpoint Publishing, 1987.

Kashrut For the 21ST Century: i.e. Vegetarianism

Rabbi Emily Faust Korzenik

Over the millennia Jews have lived among many civilizations and yet maintained their special identity. We have shown a remarkable capacity to adapt to the vastly changing conditions of our lives and at the same time maintain the essential moral and ethical thrust of Judaism and many of its civilizing traditions.

Change and new ideas are a source of vitality even as they produce tension and disequilibrium. Sometimes newly engaging and morally appealing ideas fly in the face of honored, age old traditions. Conflict within ensues. Such a new idea which emerged from the secular world of America and disturbed the core of accepted Jewish practice was the idea of equality for women, now partially resolved. Occasionally we are more fortunate and a morally appealing and beneficial idea begins to gain currency which in no way defies traditional requirements. Vegetarianism is such an idea.

Vegetarianism is compatible with kashrut. Jews are not required to eat meat, but when and if they do certain limitations apply. It must be acknowledged that the large majority of Jews do not keep kosher and would not therefore measure a dietary change against the need to maintain the laws of kashrut. However, kashrut has been a measure of serious observance among traditional Jews and one would not lightly urge upon the Jewish community practices which are contrary to Jewish tradition.

Vegetarianism is morally enlightened, healthier and economical. Children whose love for animals have not yet been overwhelmed by an acquired taste for meat are often repelled by the idea of eating an animal. When I remind myself that the neat little packages labeled beef, veal, or lamb were recently living creatures raised and killed for my gustatory pleasure, I am discomfited. If I allow truth to trouble my lifelong eating habits, images of calves confined in small cages begin to take hold. All young creatures want to run and romp, but it is standard procedure to limit the mobility of calves that are designated to become veal so that we can enjoy tender morsels.

        All animals, brainy or not, respond to the imminence of violent death with fear and trembling. When my son Joshua was 15 years old he was taken by friends in Canada to visit a slaughter house. Joshua witnessed the terror and anguished cries of the animals he saw being slaughtered and he resolved never to eat meat again. Respecting, even admiring my son's sensibilities, I set out to learn how to combine beans and brown rice, etc. That would give John the protein he needed.* More and more young people who came to our home were vegetarians. Some would eat fish and eggs; others would not. In time our whole family's eating pattern was modified. The doctors, the nutritionists, the health letters tell us all to eat less meat and more fruits and vegetables. My daughter, on purely health grounds, was refusing the meat I prepared for dinner. Each year the pot of vegetarian matzo ball soup for Passover gets larger. Reluctant to impose my evolving ways on others, I was slow to cook exclusively vegetarian meals for guests, but I recently launched my second vegetarian dinner party. Unbeknown to me one of my guests had just completed a vegetarian cooking course. Another guest has been a vegetarian for years. Granting that some would have preferred meat to my effort at innovative vegetable dishes, I'm sure no one went home hungry or with heartburn.

        Vegetarianism is more merciful and healthful and it is also more economical. I am not referring only to the fact that the cost of meals to a family is reduced. The crops we raise to feed herbivorous animals that become food for us could be used to feed many more hungry people at less cost. Soybeans commonly used to feed animals, are wonderfully nutritious for all God's creatures. In addition, environmentally harmful overgrazing of public lands would be eliminated.

The rabbis of the Talmudic period sought to make practice in their own time more perfectly expressive of the wise, holy, moral, and ethical thrust of Hebrew Scripture. The Bible tells us that we should not eat an animal that is torn of a beast or that has died of itself. The Talmudic rabbis extended those health measures with lengthy, careful explanations of how a diseased animal can be identified. Humanely, the precise sharpness of the knife used to kill an animal was prescribed. People who were disabled in ways that would prevent them from fulfilling the slaughtering requirements properly were specifically disqualified. The biblical expression of sensibility, "do not seethe the calf in the milk of its mother" moved the innovative Talmudic rabbis to the separation of milk and meat and established limitations upon the eating of meat. If a meat meal was eaten, then time must elapse before dairy could be eaten. Hunting was proscribed. A bow and arrow might maim but not necessarily kill in the swift and relatively painless way that ritual slaughtering required.

The direction that both the Bible and the Talmud set for us is clear. Now it is time to bring rachmanut (mercy) for animals to a still nobler level. Some vegetarians contend that an increase in our sensibility to the suffering we impose on animals would lead us to be kinder to humans. It was not long ago that animal protein was thought to be a dietary essential. Now we know that vegetable protein is a healthier alternative.

In these times which are so hard on all too many, there are hungry people in our own communities. At the close of the Yom Kippur fast, members of Stamford's Jewish congregations bring bags filled with groceries which are then distributed to a local food pantry. What if the Jewish community extended that mitzvah? What if every Jewish family placed a pushke (coin box) for tsedakah (charity) on the dining table and filled it each week with money saved by eating meatless meals? Still another blessing would flow from a benign, beneficial change in diet.

How much longer will we be slaves to the fleshpots when there is a more humane, healthier, and economical halacha (way to go).

* Editor's note: The idea that vegetarians must eat "complementary" foods, such as beans and rice in order to obtain sufficient protein was advanced in the early days of the vegetarian movement, and by Frances Moore Lappé in *Diet for A Small Planet*. The idea was erroneous, and Frances Moore Lappé has since rescinded it. The science of nutrition, neglected for a century and half, has advanced enormously in the past generation. In general, it is a good idea for any beginning vegetarian, to join a vegetarian organization, such as The North American Jewish Vegetarian Group, The International Jewish Vegetarian Society, Vegetarian Resource Group or North American Vegetarian Society to be educated about vegetarian nutrition and know where to find good recipes, recipe books and other material on the subject.

A Personal Statement

Rabbi Michael L. Kramer

If pressed, I don't know whether I truly understand why I've become a vegetarian. All I know is that through a series of events I found myself drifting towards vegetarianism and then into it. I know that it involves respect I feel towards my daughter, honor to my father's memory, a concern for my personal health, and a desire to live a more sanctified life, but I've had difficulty sorting out all the factors.

When my daughter, Rachel, was ten years old, I took her to a Chinese restaurant to celebrate New Year's Eve. Rachel was not an experienced Chinese *fresser* as was her father and so I ordered duck for her, but when it came, she refused to eat it. She stated that she couldn't imagine eating anything that reminded her of Donald Duck. At the time, I was a little baffled and I figured that she would get over this eccentricity, but she didn't. Instead, Rachel embarked on a life of vegetarianism. At first, I was puzzled by her decision, but soon I became proud of her determination and principles.

Several years later my wife, Barbara, also became a vegetarian. Meals in our house became difficult. My son was a stalwart meat eater. I recall, at one point when I had given up beef on my journey towards vegetarianism, I served three types of chili at dinner: one with beef, one with ground turkey, and one vegetarian. The chef at the Hard Rock Café would be proud of me.

Around four years ago my father, who at the time was rabbi emeritus at Temple Israel in Staten Island, died. During the shiva, Richard Schwartz, the author of *Judaism and*

Vegetarianism, my father's friend, paid his respects. Meeting Richard and talking to him gave me the impetus to put more thought into my decision. However, it wasn't only talking to Richard that prodded me in that direction. I think that I wanted to do something to show respect to my father or to make some sacrifice in his memory. My father, though not a vegetarian, had a reverence for life and was devoted to his community. Thinking back, I wonder whether my decision to become a vegetarian is not tied to his memory.

Another factor in my decision to turn to vegetarianism has been my health. A number of years ago I had my gall bladder removed, a result of a too rich diet as well as terrible eating habits. After becoming vegetarian, I discovered that I felt better. While indigestion was a common ailment before, I cannot remember experiencing that phenomenon since. Last year I was diagnosed with adult-onset diabetes as well as with high blood pressure. These diseases literally scared me into dieting and entering an exercise regimen to lose weight. Baruch haShem--I've managed to overcome both problems, but it has taught me a valuable lesson which has changed my eating regiment further.

As a Reform Jew, I look at *kedushah* as a process. We are never there, but always reaching. We are obligated to ask, "How can we bring greater sanctity to our lives?" I was brought up in a home that wasn't kosher, but I found myself with a desire to move in that direction. I would still not describe our home as kosher, but becoming vegetarian is a giant step in that direction. We don't have to worry about mixing *milchig* and *fleishig,* and we read labels to make sure that we are using vegetable oils instead of animal fat. Being a vegetarian also makes it less worrisome inviting kosher friends to our home.

As I moved in this direction in my life, I've occasionally discussed kashrut and vegetarianism with my confirmation students. A particular film strip on kashrut that I've shown displays the ritual slaughter of a cow by a shochet. This strip gave pause both to my students as well as myself as to whether killing an animal even for food was proper. I've studied Jewish sources in regard to vegetarianism and I am convinced that it shows a higher regard for life, and that it is what God seeks from us. Knowing that I am a vegetarian affirms for me that at least in one area in my life I am following a path of righteousness.

The Kamenitser Maggid: The Rev. C.Z. Maccoby

by E. Shoerats

Like the progress across the skies of a heavenly body of unusual brilliance and magnificence, appearing but once in a lifetime, whose splendour makes an abiding, never-to-be-forgotten memory, so was the impact created by the Rev. Chaim Zundel Maccoby, familiarly known as the Kamenitser Maggid, on the masses both here and abroad, and whose 50th anniversary of his passing occurred last year.

Commencing his career as a preacher in Russia at the early age of 16 years, his fame spread quickly even beyond the borders of the land of his birth and his work for the Chovevei Zion (Love of Zion) Movement caused it to spread rapidly among the people whose hearts were inspired by his great oratory and sincerity.

The Tzarist Government became apprehensive of his popularity; they objected to his travelling the country, making passionate appeals in support of emigration to Palestine. They considered he might be a revolutionary and as his life was in peril he escaped to England. This was fortunate for the Jewish community of this country, particularly the East End of London which he served selflessly and with unmatched zeal for the last 26 years of his all too short life, up to his passing in 1916.

Only a biography would do justice to this amazing figure; in this brief sketch one can only relate his great oratorical prowess. He could hold vast crowds who avidly listened to him, spellbound and enthralled for hours, certainly he was the greatest preacher this country had ever heard.

Moreover his learning was not limited to homiletics and the Agadie of the Talmud, which was sufficient for the purpose of most maggadim. In addition, he was a profound Rabbinic scholar in Halacha (Talmudic law) equally excelling in this field of learning. He would disentangle and clarify most abstruse and complicated points with rare skill, speaking for two hours on end, yet with unabated freshness to the conclusion of a peroration. In addition to such accomplishments he was also in possession of considerable secular knowledge. The non-Jewish world called him the Jewish Spurgeon!

For Jewish vegetarians as well as others, the Kamenitser was of special significance for he was a consistent ethical vegetarian, even dispensing with leather shoes, and substitutes were not so good then as now. When preaching he never failed to use all his persuasive powers in furtherance of the vegetarian ideal. He condemned the cruelty involved and invoked the women, at a time when the fight to survive required the greatest strength, not to lower their husbands' strength, vitality and health by feeding them on a deficient flesh diet. The Jewish press was silent on this aspect and he was no doubt unpopular with his contemporaries.

Through the good offices of a grandson of the Kamenitser, Mr. H. Pollard, of Bournemouth, I was allowed to interview his daughter, a lady around 90 years of age, shortly before her death. In her weak state I refrained from plying her with many questions, but decided to ascertain two matters:

1. "What did your father teach you children regarding meat eating?"

"Oh," she replied, "That it was cruel, cruel."

2. "What did he do about the shank bone for Seder?"
"He substituted another egg for it."

There is a daughter still living, a distinguished lady of 86, who was Vice-Headmistress of the Jews' Free School and Headmistress of the Westminster Jews' Free School before retiring. She provided a home for her parents and devoted her life to caring for them with undying love and affection. She has been a militant vegetarian all her life and took an active interest in the vegetarian movement.

Bearing this in mind it is not surprising when we read in the obituary notice that only one Rabbi from the Federation to whom the Maggid was attached attended the funeral, in addition to their President, Lord Swaythling, and a vast concourse of people who so loved him. One can understand the non-attendance of the elite Ministers of the fashionable United Synagogue of that time, but what could explain the reason for the absence of the more Orthodox Rabbonim?

There has fortunately been a wind of change in the last few years and many Rabbis of eminence have adopted vegetarianism. Others when questioned say, "We don't eat much meat" or "The time is not opportune," etc., but undoubtedly much of the compassionate and courageous thought among Jewish people today is the result of the forthright and challenging inspiration which our parents and grandparents received from Chaim Maccoby....

Extract From Sdei Chemed

Rabbi Chaim Chezkiyahu Medini
(trans. by Eli Pick) *

The following is an authoritative rabbinic (not vegetarian) statement which combats the wholely unsupportable view held by certain persons that animal eating is related to Judaism.

On the subject of eating meat nowadays, Rabbi Chaviv in the Knesset Hagedolah (Yoreh Deah, Ch. 28) writes in the name of the Rashal of blessed memory, that we many not rely on the Ri and the Ran, the medieval Rabbinic authorities, that one may eat meat for the sake of nourishment. However, Rabbi Chida writes in *Hayim Sheol,* Ch 63, section 6, "and it all depends upon the type of person, that if one can restrain oneself...how worthy that would be...." As for ourselves, how can we respond to this in our own generation of low standards, when it is impossible to stop so many sins, and we fail in being able to control ourselves, the good Lord Almighty should forgive us. Such is written by the Rabbi in *Ot Hi Leolam,* page 63, column 3. From here we find support and justification from a particularly distinguished person, highly esteemed in "body, spirit and soul," who for many years has abstained completely from consuming any meat. Woe unto those who sneer at him, and happy will be his lot! Even from wine he abstained, except for when he was performing a religious duty (e.g. Kiddush or four Cups of Passover Seder).

It is known that people work hard to feed themselves, but a number of sins result from excessive eating, or from drinking too much wine. God have mercy on us.

A number of rabbis had already written in the name of the Ari (Rabbi Isaac Luria), "Happy is the person who is able to abstain from meat and wine for the whole week." Refer, too, to the *Beair Haitav* in Orach Chayim, Ch. 134, paragraph 3 (who writes, "There is an adopted practice not to eat meat, not to drink wine, on Monday and Thursday, since the Heavenly Court is then sitting in judgement, and happy is the person who is able to refrain from meat and wine during the whole week"). Also refer to Yakhil Shlomo in Orach Chayim, Ch. 529, paragraph 2.

It is true it is written on Sabbath one dines with meat and wine, but that is specified as a person's right and not as a duty, as it says in the Talmud (Sabbath 118a), "A person should eat properly on Shabbath just as on a weekday." This is also the interpretation of the Darkei Moshe in Yoreh Deah, Ch 341. In *Reshit Chochman*, page 129, column 2, there is a lengthy discussion which concludes that one may not eat from anything which has formed part of a living creature. In *Shvet Mussar,* page 192, it says that meat is only permitted to a person who is extremely righteous, but this is only the teaching of the pious, and it is not actually prohibited for any person to eat meat. Nevertheless, we have learnt that it is correct to refrain from doing so, and if a person is able to, he is regarded as being in a high state of holiness.

See also the *Kerem Shlomo* in Yoreh Deah, Ch 1, who amplifies to explain that there is no duty to a person to consume meat or wine, even on Sabbaths and Festivals.

I have now come across the Kabbalistic work *Shiur Komah* of the *Ramak,* and my devoted pupils have shown to me page 84, column 3, regarding the transmigration of the soul of the wicked into an animal. A conscientious person will distance himself from eating any animal flesh, as it is possible that the soul of a wicked person clings to the animal right until its death. This could have a bad influence over the person who consumes the animal's flesh. The proof-reader has added there that in the light of this, a person should never eat meat unless old secrets have been revealed to him to determine whether there is any evil person's soul couched within the animal. A similar warning is given by the Ari (Rabbi Isaac Luria) in the *Sefer Hamitzvot Parashat Ekev,* that for this reason one should never eat much meat. He adds that one must certainly never eat the heart of any animal, beast or bird, as therein lies the prime endowment of life.

* Ed. Note. Rabbi Medini was born in Jerusalem in 1832. He studied in Istanbul, then became a prominent rabbi and teacher in Southern Russia, where he founded many Yeshivot academies. He returned to settle in Hebron, where he was appointed head of the religious court. He died in 1904.

Vegetarianism: An Orthodox Jewish Perspective

Rabbi David Rosen

It behooves an Orthodox Rabbi, in particular, to argue a case for or against a particular practice on the basis of Jewish law, halacha. Indeed, I believe that there are compelling halachic reasons as well as meta-halachic reasons for advocating vegetarianism.

Any halachic argument cannot deny that Judaism does allow for the consumption of meat. Yet of course it does so under very controlled conditions and criteria. These refer not only to the way in which the animal is slaughtered, but also concern the treatment of the animal up until that moment. However, even if there have been times and places when these standards may have been met, the current treatment of animals in the livestock trade definitely renders the consumption of meat as halachically unacceptable as the product of illegitimate means.

Moreover, the stringent ethical demands made not only of the shochet but also of anyone wishing to consume meat especially after the destruction of the Temple, led the Talmud itself and notable medieval authorities to encourage abstinence from meat eating (see Babylonian Talmud, Pesachim 49b and 108a; Rabbi Elijah de Vidas, Reshit Chochma 4, 129; Rabbi Yehuda Ashkenazi (Be'er Heitev) quotes Isaac Luria (the "Ari") in Shulchan Aruch Orah Haim, sect. 134)

Indeed, a central precept regarding the relationship between humans and animals in halacha, is the prohibition of causing cruelty to animals---Tsa'ar ba'alei chayim. As mentioned, practices in the livestock trade today constitute a flagrant violation of this prohibition. I refer not only to the most obvious and outrageous of these, such as the production of veal and goose liver, but also to common practices in the livestock trade such as hormonal treatment and massive drug dosing.

Furthermore, the retention of these hormones and drugs which are pumped into livestock pose a threat to human health together with the concentration of toxins at the end of the food chain contained in animal flesh. As it is halachically prohibited to harm oneself and as healthy nutritious vegetarian alternatives are easily available, meat consumption has become halachically unjustifiable.

However, as important as it is to address the halachic issues, the religious Jew must always be conscious of the goal of halachic conduct, the teleology of Torah (see Nachmanides on Leviticus ch. 19, v. 1).

As Rabbi Avraham Yitzhak HaCohen Kook pointed out, not only are the ideal societal images in the Tanach the Garden of Eden and the Messianic age--vegetarian societies; but the very language with which meat eating is permitted is concessionary--"if your soul *lusts* to eat meat" (Deuteronomy ch. 12 v.20)--not ideal.

The explicit purpose of the Biblical dietary laws is holiness (Leviticus Ch. 11 v. 44) and our sages declared in relation to these, that "the mitzvot were only given in order to purify (ennoble) people." Maimonides and Abarbanel, quoting the midrash on Leviticus chapter 17 v. 7, saw the sacrifices as laid down in the Torah, as a concession to the forms of religious practice at the time and as designed to wean the children of Israel away from paganism. As the mitzvot are intended to ennoble us, and as the ideal images of the Torah are vegetarian, it is natural to similarly see the laws of kashrut (as does Rabbi Kook) as actually designed to wean us away from meat eating towards the vegetarian ideal.

Today not only are we able to enjoy a healthy balanced vegetarian diet as perhaps never before; and not only are there in fact the above mentioned compelling halachic reasons for not eating meat; but above all, if we strive for that which Judaism aspires to--namely the ennoblement of the spirit, then a vegetarian diet becomes a moral imperative--the authentic Jewish ethical dietary way of life for our times and for all time.

In his Mishneh Torah (Code of Jewish Law), in the section, "Foundations of the Torah" (Chapter 2 Mishnah 2) Maimonides explains how the all-encompassing Biblical precept to love God, may be observed. Through studying and meditating upon the beauty and wonder of Creation, he states, we draw closer to the very Source of all.

In other words, the love of God is expressed through our love and respect of Creation. While undoubtedly for Judaism, there is a hierarchy in the Creation in which the human being is at the summit, nevertheless, evidently the more sensitive and respectful we are towards God's Creation, in particular God's creatures, the more respectful and reverential we actually are towards God.

Indeed, Judaism as a way of life, seeks to inculcate in us a consciousness of the Divine Presence in the World and respect for life accordingly. The more we care for life, the closer we are in fact to God. Accordingly, an ethical vegetarian way of life expresses the most noble and sublime values and aspirations of Judaism itself, bringing us closer to its ideal vision for society as a whole.

New Year Message, 1988

At the heart of Jewish affirmation and purpose are the concepts of the love and reverence of God. The practical expression thereof is discussed by Maimonides in his Mishneh Torah, in the second chapter of Hilchot Yesodei HaTorah in the following words: "...how is the way to (fulfill the commandment) to love (God) and revere Him? When a person considers His works and His wonderful and great creations and will be in awe of His wisdom which is beyond estimation and limitation, he immediately (comes) to know the Lord."

Thus it is precisely through His creation and Creatures, that we can come to live, to truly know God.

But the love, reverence, and knowledge of the Creator are meant to lead us further. This is made clear by Maimonides in his Sefer HaMitzvot. He commences his enumeration of the commandments with the foundational precepts of Jewish faith, before dealing with all the other mitzvot. After the aforementioned principles of belief, love and reverence of God, he lists the commandments to serve God; to follow and associate with those who serve Him; to swear in His Name; and then the commandment to be God-like and imitate His ways. The ultimate implication of this leads to the concluding commandment in this section of first principles--to sanctify God's name.

However, how are we to fulfill the commandment to imitate God, to walk in His ways, on a regular daily basis?

Maimonides explains with a quotation from our sages, "Just as the Holy One Blessed be He is merciful--so you be merciful; the Holy One Blessed be He is called gracious--so you be gracious; the Holy One Blessed be His Name is righteous--so you be righteous; the Holy One Blessed be He ('s way) is lovingkindess, so your way be lovingkindness (Sifre on Deuteronomy 11, 22)...(the commandment requires us) to imitate the good deeds and honorable attributes by which the Exalted One is described through metaphor."

A further reference in this regard is to be found in Maimonides' Mishneh Torah, Hilchot Mlachim 10, 12 in relation to Jewish-Gentile relations. Maimonides quotes the Sages this time to the effect that one must be charitable to gentile poor, etc. "because of 'ways of peace', for it is said 'God is good to all, and His mercies are upon all His creatures' (Psalm 145)" and it is said "Her ways are pleasant ways and all her paths are peace (Proverbs 3)."

Furthermore in Hilchot Avadim 9, 8, Maimonides emphasizes the obligation to treat servants with kindness and compassion, and to behave with such qualities also to animal life. "The Sages of old," comments Maimonides, "would give their animals and servants to eat before their own meals"...True Jews, he continues, are "merciful towards all. And so concerning the attributes of the Holy One Blessed be He that we are commanded to emulate, it says 'and His mercies are upon all His Creatures'; and everyone who is merciful, is treated with mercy, as it is said 'and He will grant you mercy and have compassion on you and will multiply you.'"

Accordingly we may understand and paraphrase the quintessential message of Jewish Faith as follows

True love of God means awareness of His presence in His Creation. True consciousness of His presence in His Creation means care and compassion for His Creatures. The greater our sensitivity towards His Creatures the more we emulate His Attributes, ennoble our world and sanctify His Name--the very metier of our existence.

Aside from the fact that both the original Garden of Eden and the Messianic vision of the future reflect the vegetarian ideal in Judaism, it is of course such a dietary lifestyle that is most consonant with the goal and purpose of Torah to maximise our awareness, appreciation and sensitivity to the Divine Presence in the world. It is therefore only natural for us to affirm as did Rav Kuk, the first Ashkenazi Chief Rabbi in Israel, that a Redeemed World must perforce be a vegetarian world.

The Torah And Flesh Eating: Shechitah and Anti Semitism
December, 1989

Many halachic sources make it clear that the statement advocating meat eating as an expression of religious celebration is not mandatory but permissive, and that indeed if one finds such to be physically and or morally repulsive it would be very wrong to do so. (see specifically Kerem Shlomo Yoreh Deah, 1; Yakhel Shlomo, Orach Chayim 529 (2); Reshit Chochman 129b; see also other sources brought in vol. 6 (ref. "basar") of Sdei Chemed advocating total abstinence from meat eating).

Perhaps the most powerful argument in favor of vegetarianism for God fearing Jews today more than ever before, is Rabbi Berkovitz's most forceful point in his rallying call against anti-shechitah legislation--namely the prohibition against "Chillul Hashem," the desecration of God's name.

Surely it is precisely such a desecration when observant Jews eat animals produced and treated under conditions of cruelty that flagrantly flout Jewish teaching and prohibitions concerning "Tza'ar Ba'alei Chayim." Is it anything less than a "Chillul Hashem" to declare veal for example, which is produced through wanton human cruelty to a calf, to be Kasher, simply because at points "Y" and "Z" the animal was slaughtered and prepared in accordance with halachic dictates, after the commandments affecting human responsibility towards animal life have been desecrated from points "A" to "X?"

Most people of course are simply ignorant or intentionally ignorant of the manifold transgressions involved in meat eating. Today's concept of Kashrut is more permeated with crass indulgence and economic exploitation than the ennoblement of the human spirit which our sages declare to be its purpose.

Today as never before, the cruelty in livestock trade renders meat eating and true Kashrut incompatible (aside from the fact that the consumption of hormones and antibiotics injected and retained in the flesh and the concentration of toxins at the end of the food chain that then pass in to the body is hardly in keeping with the commandment to care for one's physical health!).

If meat eating were a mitzvah--an obligation--it would today in most cases be at best a "mitzvah haba'ah b'averah" or rather "b'averot"--i.e. rendered illegitimate by illegitimate means.

How much more illegitimate then is meat eating today when it is not a mandatory obligation anyway.

However, I do agree with Rabbi Berkovitz that to allow a ban of Shechita would be a "chillul hashem" if other means of slaughtering animals are allowed.

Such hypocrisy is often a thinly veiled guise for far less

than "civilized" sentiments directed against Jews and our Heritage, and Jewish vegetarians must also fight such hypocrisy. But at the same time we must clearly advocate dietary practices that are truly in consonance with the sublimest values of the Torah, and today more than ever before these are overwhelmingly incompatible with carnivorous indulgence.

On the Temple Sacrifices
June, 1990

It is surely nothing less than crass hypocrisy for those who indulge their carnivorous lusts and thereby also help maintain the barbarities in the livestock trade, etc. (much of which did not exist in Temple times) to turn up their noses at the Temple service where sacrifices were at least offered up to God in the form of spiritual devotion of the time and culture, before being partaken of as food.

However, the Orthodox Jewish vegetarian will often point to the Midrash in Vayikra Rabbah and further to Maimonides who declare animal offerings to have been born out of a concession to the forms of spiritual devotion at the time and context, but to have been replaced primarily by prayer as a higher level of devotion.

Moreover, the Temple service, as it is laid down, can be maintained without animal sacrifice. Indeed, Rabbi Kuk's vision of a vegetarian society in the Messianic Age draws support from the Rabbinic comment that "in the future all sacrifices will be abolished except for the meal offering."

I must acknowledge that such efforts to view vegetarianism within a *halachic* framework in the context of Messianic expectation cannot avoid the obligation of the paschal lamb (*Korban Pesach*).

As far as that is concerned, the legitimate response of the Orthodox Jewish vegetarian is that "I will wait to hear and do what the Messiah wills me to!" (Undoubtedly we will have our own expectation in that regard!).

In consonance with the above, I do not believe that we need to understand the liturgical passages...as expressing our hope for the restoration of animal sacrifice. These texts are above all and essentially a recognition on our part of the devotion and dedication to God that our ancestors showed in their own way. Accordingly we express our hope that we may show the same spirit of devotion and dedication to Him, in our own way.

Indeed, the language of the liturgy easily facilitates such an interpretation.

I quote from the Sabbath Musaph Amidah:

"And we shall perform and offer up before You in love, an additional Sabbath offering according to the command of Your will, just as (or "just like") you wrote down for us to do in your Torah (communicated) via Moses by the (direct) utterance of Your glory, as it is stated: and on the Sabbath day you shall offer up, etc., etc."

The phrase "just as" or "just like" can mean "the same" or "similar"--in quality and devotion, for example, but not necessarily in the same form!

If we understand the text in this way, then the recitation of the sacrificial specifications is, as I have mentioned, but to record the devotion of the past, to inspire us to devotion to God in different forms and ways in the present and future.

This is the way I understand the text and the way I pray when reciting such texts.

Please note that Judaism demands of us to pray with "kavanah," sincere intention, and thus requires our own personal undertakings of the statutory texts that we are obliged to recite.

If we do not do this, then inevitably we are guilty of praying by rote/automatically, which our Sages condemn and warn us against strongly.

Ethical Vegetarianism: The Perspective Of A Reform Jew

Rabbi Edward Rosenthal

Introduction

New Zealand is one of those places that is usually forgotten about in high school geography. In fact, it is a small country (about the size of Colorado) made up of two major islands in the lower portion of the South Pacific, with a population of about 3,500,000 people (and 80,000,000 sheep!)

While preparing to take up my position as the Rabbi of Beth Shalom in Auckland, I spent many hours contemplating the endless variations of how to cook New Zealand lamb and mutton. When, to my great surprise, I learned that deer is farm-raised like sheep and cattle in New Zealand, my mind raced with the thought of kosher venison. I was certain that with so much livestock, the cost of kosher meat would undoubtedly be less than that to which I had become accustomed in Cincinnati.

Upon arrival I was met with the sad reality of the situation. In the entire country there is only one *shochet,* who lived in the capital city of Wellington at the bottom of the North Island, 660 kilometers from Auckland. After the animals are slaughtered in Wellington, the meat is frozen and shipped around the country. The quality was poor and the price approximately four times that of non-kosher meat. Confronted by this predicament, rather than eat such poor quality kosher meat, I simply decided to stop eating meat altogether.

Initially, it could not be said that I became a vegetarian, for to become a vegetarian requires a conscious, positive choice. My decision to refrain from meat was not positive. It was a reaction to circumstances which were beyond my control. Having been a devout carnivore, it was no easy task to stop eating meat. However, four years later, after a great deal of study, I can now say that I am a vegetarian.

Like most *baalei teshuvah,* I believe strongly in my convictions. My wife (who has been a vegetarian since 1979) continually reminds me that Reform Judaism and fanaticism do not mix. As always, she is correct. There is no room for fanaticism in Reform Judaism, and vegetarians (unjustly so) are often thought to be fanatics. However, Reform Judaism and vegetarianism do mix.

Particularistic and Ethical Mitzvot

Modern Reform Judaism has seen a swing back to many traditional observances. Yet with regard to the observance of particularistic mitzvot, Reform Judaism has always accepted the right of the individual to choose those which add meaning to one's life. Thus, for example, there are many Reform Jews today who observe at least some degree of kashrut: from biblical kashrut out of the home to full rabbinic kashrut observed in many Reform households. The autonomous individual hopefully, through a commitment to study and learning, makes educated choices to observe these *mitzvot* as a means to enhance his/her life, but Reform Judaism has never stated that such observance is obligatory upon any Reform Jew.

In the case of ethical mitzvot, however, Reform Judaism from its inception has accepted them as having been given by God and binding upon all Jews. Even as autonomous individuals, we do not have the right to choose which ethical *mitzvot* can be observed and which cannot. As a Reform Jew, one cannot choose whether to observe, "Thou shalt not commit murder" and ignore "Thou shalt not commit adultery" or "Thou shalt not steal." Through all of the developments which have taken place, that which has not changed is the unequivocal belief of Reform Judaism that the ethical and moral laws of the Torah are binding and obligatory. Indeed, Reform Judaism can and still does call itself ethical, prophetic Judaism.

Vegetarianism: The Original Dietary Laws

"And God said: Behold, I have given you every herb yielding seed, which is upon the face of all the earth, and every tree in which is the fruit of a tree yielding seed--to you it shall be for food." (Gen: 1:29).

It is quite clear that in the Edenic state, Adam and Eve did not consume the flesh of other animals for food. This view is presented in the Talmud,[1] as well as by Rashi,[2] Ibn Ezra,[3] Ramban,[4] Cassuto[5] and Rav Kook, [6] amongst others. It is this pristine state of human existence about which we reminisce and dream: a time when there was no hatred, no disease, no famine and no war--when humans were free and uninhibited, when there was no knowledge of good and evil and everything was right. It is this same state for which we hope in *yemot haMashiach.* We wait for the time when the world will come full circle to that state of pure peace which is characterized in the first chapter of Genesis.

Of course, the state of Edenic perfection could not last. After being expelled from *Gan Eden,* the progeny of Adam and Eve sank quickly to a level of violence and immorality which bore no resemblance to paradise. So low did humans sink that God could tolerate them no more: "And God said unto Noah: The end of all flesh is come before Me; for the earth is filled with violence through them; and behold, I will destroy them with the earth." (Gen. 6:13). Even in the new order following the Flood, it became all too clear that with free will, humans were too weak to make the moral sacrifice of not eating other creatures. This concession to human weakness is found in Genesis 9:2-3:

> "The dread of you and the terror of you shall be upon every animal of the earth, and upon every fowl of the heaven, upon all that creeps upon the ground and upon all the fish of the sea; into your hand are they given. Every creeping thing that lives shall be food for you; as the green herb have I given you all things."

While Genesis 9 does give human beings permission to eat meat, there is no doubt that God allowed this as a concession to human weakness. Nehama Leibowitz explains this concession stating that,

> "...after the Deluge, the descendants of Noah, that is, all mankind, were permitted to be carnivorous. Since the land had become filled with violence and man had given free rein to his worst instincts, man was no longer required to make the supreme moral exertions required to forego the slaughter of animals. It was far more important that he should, at least, utilize what moral fibre he still possessed in refraining from killing his own kind and respecting the life of his neighbor.[7]

In other words, God allowed humans to kill and eat animals in an effort to keep them from killing each other. The only restriction placed upon animal consumption was the Noachite law (Gen. 9:4) which forbade the eating of blood: "But flesh with its soul, that is the blood, you shall not eat."

Clearly, permission to eat flesh was a Divine concession. Recognizing that humans were incapable of mastering their violent tendencies, the Torah allows them to vent their passions and assert dominion over all those creatures for whom they previously served as caretakers and protectors. The prohibition against eating blood is the last barrier to keep humans from becoming inhuman; to remove the blood is the minimum requirement of humane treatment. Thus, the state of affairs preceding the Flood represents the direct antithesis to the perfection of *Gan Eden*, and the new order following the flood was based upon a concession to human weakness.

Kashrut as Compromise

What has been shown to this point is the universal culinary history of humankind as presented in the Torah, from vegetarian perfection in the Garden of Eden to wanton gluttony following the Flood. With God's selection of the Jewish people, it became necessary to separate the Jews from the other peoples of the earth. This, of course, was achieved through *mitzvot*. With regard to dietary *mitzvot,* while the rest of the world refrained only from eating blood, the Jews were commanded to refrain from particular classses of food. What was acceptable for others was now forbidden to Jews.

Any effort to rationalize or explain 'reasons' for the laws of *kashrut* will fall short. Traditionally, the only reason to observe *kashrut* is because God has commanded us. As the Chosen People, the *mitzvot* were given to help raise that which was considered to be ordinary and profane to a level of holiness. The laws of *kashrut* serve as God's compromise to our human weakness, while trying to make us a holy people.

With this compromise, God acknowledged that humans were not yet able to achieve the perfection originally intended for them. Yet by the same token they should not be given a free rein to slaughter and eat anything which walks, crawls, slithers, hops, flies or swims. Consequently, by causing an awareness of and consideration for the life which is taken to create food, the laws of *kashrut* have brought the Jewish people half-way back to Edenic perfection.

Vegetarianism as an Ethical Mitzvah

If, as has been shown, *kashrut* is a compromise by which the character of the Jewish People was honed in order to distinguish us from the other nations of the world, then, from a Reform perspective, this is a particularistic *mitzvah.* Thus, like kindling fire on shabbat or separating shatness, it should be left to the individual, through study and examination, to find personal and spiritual meaning. If, on the other hand, vegetarianism is the universal, ethical law of human food consumption, then it is this form of *'kashrut'* which the Reform Jew must examine.

For the Jewish vegetarian there are three main components which prove vegetarianism to be an ethical mitzvah: tsaar baalei haim, pikuah nefesh and bal tashchit.

Tsaar Baalei Haim

As Jews, we are commanded in the Torah and throughout our tradition to show compassion to animals. *Tsaar Baalei Haim* is the injunction not to cause 'pain to living creatures.' In Psalm 145:9 we are told "The Eternal is good to all, and God's tender mercies are over all creatures." The counterpart of this verse is proverbs 12:15: "The righteous person regards the life of his beast." Maimonides explains the dictum in the *Guide for the Perplexed* 3:17--"It is set down with a view to perfecting us so that we should not acquire moral habits of cruelty and should not inflict pain gratuitously without any utility, but that we should intend to be kind and merciful even with a chance animal."[8] Indeed, a righteous person cannot intentionally be cruel to an animal, yet even the righteous can unwittingly become complacent to their suffering.[9]

Who would not rebuke a child for abusing a puppy or for pulling the wings off a butterfly and not take the opportunity to teach that child about *tsaar baalei haim?* Yet on the same day that child might be fed veal chops or roasted chicken for dinner. The torment and cruelty which so many animals undergo in the process of becoming food is astounding. In his book, *Judaism and Vegetarianism,* Dr. Richard Schwartz tells of what goes into the raising of veal for food:

> After being allowed to nurse for only one or two days, the veal calf is removed from its mother, with no consideration of its need for motherly nourishment, affection, and physical contact. The calf is locked in a small slatted stall without enough space to move around, stretch, or even lie down. To obtain the pale, tender veal desired by consumers, the calf is purposely kept anaemic by giving it a special high-calorie, iron-free diet. The calf craves iron so much that it would lick the iron fittings on its stalls and its own urine if permitted to do so; it is prevented from turning by having its head tethered to the stall. The stall is kept very warm and the calf is not given any water, so that it will drink more of

its high-calorie liquid diet. The very unnatural conditions of the veal calf---its lack of exercise, sunlight, fresh air, proper food and water and any emotional stimulation--make for a very sick, anaemic animal. Antibiotics and drugs are used to keep the calf from becoming ill. The calf leaves its pen only when taken for slaughter; sometimes it drops dead from the exertion of going to slaughter.[10]

Dr. Schwartz also explains the making of paté de foie gras, of which Israel is today one of the world's leading exporters. Says Dr. Schwartz:

> There is tremendous cruelty in the forced feeding of ducks and geese to produce paté de foie gras. Foie gras literally means "fat liver." The liver of a goose or duck is fattened by having 60-80 pounds of corn inserted by force down its gullet. The farmer generally holds the neck of the goose between his legs, pouring the corn with one hand and massaging it down the neck with the other. When this process is no longer effective, a wooden plunger is used to compact it still further. The bird suffers unimaginable pain, and the liver grows to an enormous size; sclerosis of the liver develops. Finally, after 25 days of such agony, when the bird is completely stupefied with pain and unable to move, it is killed and the gigantic liver, considered a delicacy, is removed. Currently machines are used to force-feed birds to make the process more efficient, with greater resultant agony.[11]

The cruelty which so permeates the meat industry is not limited to veal and foie gras, but extends to virtually every type of flesh food which is eaten by humans. 'Factory farming' is the term used to describe the methods of raising animals for food. Under the conditions of factory farming the animals are not treated as living beings created by God, but rather as inanimate objects with neither life nor soul which can be treated with whatever cruelty is necessary to be efficient and cost-effective. Factory farming is a blatant violation of the ethical mitzvah of *tsaar baalei haim.*

Pikkuah Nefesh

Based upon Leviticus 19:16---"You shall not stand idly while thy neighbor bleeds "pikkuah nefesh" is the ethical *mitzvah* to have regard for human life. So great is this *mitzvah* that Shabbat can be violated in order to save a life (Yoma 85b). Yet if *pikkuah nefesh* is the regard for human life, then what role does it play in vegetarianism which has regard for animal life?

It is erroneously believed that vegetarians only have regard for animal life and put the life of an animal over that of a human. In fact, ethical vegetarians believe that if one considers the life of an animal, then that person will be even more likely to consider the life of a fellow human being.

Pikkuah Nefesh is not only the regard for human life which is in immediate danger. *Safek sakhant nefashot* is concern for a person indirectly endangered by a condition of health which, though not serious, might deteriorate and consequently endanger life.

It is a fact that the two highest killer diseases in the United States today are heart disease and cancer. It is estimated that approximately 4,000 people die from these two diseases alone every day in the United States. Yet as early as 1961, the *Journal of the American Medical Association* said: "Ninety to ninety-seven percent of heart disease can be prevented by a vegetarian diet."[12] Twenty-one years later in September of 1982, doctors at the National Cancer Institute said, "Changing the way we eat could offer some protection against cancer. The first guideline is to reduce fat. The second is to increase the amount of fruit and vegetables. The National Cancer Institute has now made diet its number-one area of research in cancer prevention.[13] When the National Cancer Institute speaks of reducing fat, it means in particular a reduction in saturated fats. Ironically, traditional Ashkenazic Jewish cooking--*gedempteh* chicken, chopped liver, *kreplach, cholent,* etc.--is full of saturated fats.

It is commonly believed that human beings are natural carnivores and consequently need meat in order to stay healthy and strong. According to this way of thinking, to refrain from eating meat would threaten one's health and consequently become *sakkanat nefashot*. However, Dr. William Clifford Roberts, Editor-in-Chief of the *American Journal of Cardiology,* stated in a recent editorial that this is an erroneous belief. Said Dr. Roberts: "Although we think we are one and we act as if we are one, human beings are not natural carnivores. When we kill animals to eat them, they end up killing us because their flesh, which contains cholesterol and saturated fat, was never intended for human beings, who are natural herbivores."[14]

Saturated fats and cholesterol unfortunately are not the only threats to good health. The amount of chemicals injected and ingested into an animal before, during and after its life on this earth are staggering. This point is clarified by Gary and Steven Null: "The animals are kept alive and fattened by continuous administration of tranquilizers, hormones, antibiotics and 2,700 other drugs. The process starts even before birth and continues long after death. Although these drugs will still be present in the meat when you eat it, the law does not require that they be listed on the package."[15]

Anyone who ever attended junior high school biology classes knows that when an animal dies its flesh begins to putrefy and decay. After a few days the flesh turns a sickly grey-green color and produces a foul stench. The meat industry masks this natural process of decay by adding nitrites and nitrates to preserve the healthy, red look of freshly dead meat. This artificial process could be termed 'culinary embalming.'

For the Jewish vegetarian such a diet is *safek sakkanat nefashot* and poses an imminent threat to human life. By eliminating the saturated fats, cholesterol and chemicals which are found in flesh food diets and by increasing our consumption of fruits and vegetables, we eliminate the *sakkanat nefashot* and fulfill the ethical *mitzvah* of *pikkuah nefesh*. A vegetarian diet leads to the fulfillment of this ethical *mitzvah*.

Bal Tashchit

Based upon Deuteronomy 20:19---"When in your war against a city you have to besiege it for a long time in order to capture it, you must not destroy its trees."---*bal tashchit* is the law which prohibits waste. In his commentary on this verse, Rabbi Samson Raphael Hirsch states: "The legal concept of *bal tashchit* is defined as a prohibition against the purposeless, wasteful destruction of any object. Thus the concept of *bal tashchit* becomes an all-encompassing warning to man not to misuse his assigned station in the world by destroying the things of earth capriciously, in a fit of violence or even just thoughtlessly.[16]

How many Reform rabbis deliver sermons about the need to fight world hunger? How many Reform synagogues collect food for the hungry? How many Reform youth groups work to clean up the pollution which surrounds us? What conscientious Reform Jew would say that to fight world hunger and to clean up our global environment are not uses of social action which should be at the top of the agenda for Reform Judaism?

In her book, Diet for a Small Planet, Frances Moore Lappé asks us to picture ourselves seated at a table in front of an eight-ounce steak. "Then imagine the room filled with 45 to 50 people with empty bowls in front of them. For the 'feed cost' of your steak, each of their bowls could be filled with a full cup of cooked cereal grains."[17] According to information compiled by the United States Department of Agriculture, over 90 percent of all the grain produced in America goes to feed livestock that eventually wind up on dinner tables.[18]

With millions of people dying of starvation and malnutrition every year around the world, can it be perceived as anything but the most flagrant violation of *bal tashchit* to use 16 pounds of edible grains and soybeans to produce one pound of beef? As early as 1977, noted nutritionist Dr. Jean Mayer estimated that by reducing the world meat production only ten percent, enough grain would be available to feed sixty million people.[19]

The other problems created by the meat industry which

violate *bal tashchit* are the immense pollution and destruction of the environment which it produces. Today, for the sake of more land space to graze cattle, the earth's tropical rain forests are being bulldozed at a rate of 100 acres per minute. At that rate, the rain forests will be gone by the middle of the next century. Since the rain forests serve as the earth's air-conditioning or cooling system, their destruction is one of the leading causes of global warming.

Water, once taken for granted, is another victim of a meat-centered diet. Livestock in America produce about 2 billion tons of waste annually. Literally, mountains of manure wash into our streams, rivers and underground water sources. This waste is more than ten times that produced by humans. At the same time slaughterhouses serve as another tremendous source of pollution. One study showed that the 18 meat packing companies in Omaha, Nebraska discharge daily 100,000 pounds of grease, carcass dressing, carcass cleaning, intestinal waste, paunch manure, and fecal matter from viscera into the sewer system that empties into the Missouri River.

When the effects of the meat industry on our environment are considered, coupled with the tremendous waste of edible grain used to feed livestock instead of feeding the hungry, a meat-based diet is clearly a violation of *bal tashchit.*

Conclusion

Four years ago I stopped eating meat. By studying the Jewish attitudes towards vegetarianism I hoped to prove to myself that this strange way of eating was contrary to Jewish tradition. I had been taught that since the eating of meat was permitted, it would be wrong not to partake of it. For when push came to shove, I truly enjoyed a good steak: medium-rare, covered with cracked pepper, sprinkled with a bit of curry and cooked over an open flame. However, sincere and open-minded examination of the issue prevents disregard of what the tradition teaches. This article has reviewed only the surface of what is a very complex, ethical issue relevant for our times and certainly for the future of our world.

Finally, the most practical question of all. As a former meat-eater, was it hard to give up that which was so near and dear to my heart (literally)? The answer is Yes! Yet, if I enjoyed eating meat so much, why stop? The best way to answer that is by comparison. Would I like to be a millionaire? Yes. Would I be prepared to steal a million dollars to satisfy my desire? No! As a Reform Jew, I understand 'Thou shalt not steal' as an ethical *mitzvah* which is given by God. To violate that ethical *mitzvah*, for me, would be a sin. So too, when I go to a barbecue and smell the beautiful fragrance emanating from what is being cooked, do I desire to partake of it? Sometimes. Would I be prepared to satisfy that desire? No! As a Reform Jew, I understand "Behold, I have given you every herb yielding seed, which is upon the face of all the earth, and every tree in which is the fruit of a tree yielding seed --to you it shall be for food" as an ethical *mitzvah* which is given by God. To violate that ethical *mitzvah*, for me, would be a sin.

As a Reform Jew, I cannot ignore my understanding of vegetarianism as an ethical *mitzvah*, an ethical *mitzvah* which commands me not to kill another living, sentient creature. An ethical *mitzvah* which commands me to preserve and protect human life, not harm or destroy it by filling my body with harmful fats and chemicals. An ethical *mitzvah* which commands me not to waste food which could be used to feed starving children, by feeding it to livestock destined for the slaughterhouse. An ethical *mitzvah* which commands me to protect and maintain, not contribute to the wholesale destruction of our global environment; for this world is a gift which cannot be replaced.

NOTES

[1] Babylonian Talmud, *Sanhedrin* 59b. "Rav Judah said in Rav's name: Adam was not permitted to eat flesh, for it is written, [Behold I have given you all the herbs, etc.] 'To you it shall be for food, and to all the beasts of the earth,' implying that the beasts of the earth shall not be for you. But with the advent of the sons of Noah, it was permitted."

2 Rashi on Genesis 1:29. "Scripture places cattle and beasts on a level with them (human beings) with regard to food and does not permit Adam to kill any creature and eat its flesh, but all alike were to eat herbs."

3 Ibn Ezra on Genesis 1:29. "At this point flesh was not permitted (for eating) until after the flood."

4 Ramban on Genesis 1:29 "Meat was not permitted to them until the time of the Sons of Noah."

5 Cassuto on Genesis 1:27 in *From Adam to Noah*, p. 58, quoted from N. Leibowitz, *Studies in Bereshit*, (Jerusalem: World Zionist Organization, 1981), p. 77. "You are permitted to use the animals and employ them for work, have dominion over them in order to utilise their services for your subsistence, but must not hold their life cheap nor slaughter them for food. Your natural diet is vegetarian."

6 Rav Kook's writings on vegetarianism in Judaism are extensive; see *Fragments of Light: A View As To The Reasons for The Commandments* found in Ben Zion Bokser, Abraham Isaac Kook (New York, Paulist Press, 1978), pp. 303-323.

7 N. Leibowitz, *Studies in Bereshit* (Jerusalem: World Zionist Organization, 1981), p. 77.

8 Moses Maimonides, *Guide for the Perplexed*, trans. S. Pines, (Chicago: University of Chicago, 1963), p. 473.

9 The Babylonia Talmud, Baba Metzia 85a, recounts the following story about Yehuda Hanasi: "A calf was being taken to the slaughter, when it broke away, hid its head under Rabbi's cloak, and bellowed [in terror]. 'Go,' said he, for this were you created.' Thereupon they said of him [in heaven], 'Since he has not pity, let us bring suffering upon him."

10 R. Schwartz, *Judaism and Vegetarianism*, (Marblehead, MA: Micah Press, 1988), p. 77.

11 Ibid.

12 J.H. Tolbott, "Diet and Stress in Vascular Disease," *Journal of the American Medical Association*, Vol. 176, No 9 (June 1961), pp. 806-807.

13 H. Diamond and M. Diamond, *Fit for Life*, (Sydney, Australia: Angus & Robertson), p. 64.

14 W. C. Roberts, "We Think We Are One, We Act As If We Are One, But We Are Not One," *American Journal of Cardiology*, vol. 66, no. 10 (Oct., 1990), p. 896.

15 G. Null & S. Null, *How To Get Rid Of The Poisons In Your Body*,

(New York: Arco Press, 1977), p. 52.

[16] S. R. Hirsch, *Trumath Tzvi*, ed. E. Pratz, (New York: The Judaica Press, Inc., 1986), pp. 742-743.

[17] F. M. Lappé, *Diet For A Small Planet*, (New York: Ballantine Books, 1975), p. 235.

[18] Ibid., p. 12.

[19] J. Mayer, *"Dietary Goals for The United States,"* U.S. Senate Select Committee on Nutrition and Human Needs, Washington, DC, (Feb. 1977), p. 44.

Foreword to Vegetarianism & The Jewish Tradition by Louis Berman

Rabbi Zalman Schachter-Shalomi

In this book, Dr. Louis Berman maintains that vegetarianism can draw much inspiration and support from the Hebrew Bible and from rabbinical thought. I would like to endorse his thesis.

When food-conscious people wring their hands about the burdensome costs of modern technology, frequently the topic is pollution, harmful additives, or over-refined foods. I would like to point to two other unwanted side-effects of modern technology, and show how vegetarianism counteracts them.

Large-scale agriculture, modern transportation, and food processing make it possible to eat the same foods all year 'round, thus blurring our awareness of the changing seasons. Awareness of the passage of time is an important aspect of Jewish life. Pesach begins on the night of the full moon of the vernal equinox. Succoth begins on the night of the full moon of the autumnal equinox. Our sages speak of summer foods and winter foods. The *karpas* of Pesach and the *tsimmis* of *Rosh Ha'shana* symbolize the time of the year as well as the theme of the holiday. Professor Heschel put it beautifully when he said that as Jews we live more in time than we live in space. In today's world, a vegetarian keeps in closer touch with the cycle of seasons than a meat-eater.

Modern life separates man not only from the seasons of

the year, but from the sick (who are sent off to medical centers), from the old (who are hidden away in nursing homes), from the mentally incompetent (who are likewise "put away"), and also from the suffering of slaughtered animals, which is now likely to occur thousands of miles away from where a chicken or a pound of hamburger is purchased at the supermarket, prewrapped in the same clear plastic and white tray as an eggplant or bunch of broccoli. When our grandmother brought a live chicken to the *shochet,* she witnessed a sacred and skillful act intended to minimize the distress that is felt by both the victim and the meat-eater when an animal is killed for food. By direct observation she was thus qualified to transmit to her family the sentiment that, unlike everything else on the table, animal food comes to a Jewish table as a special dispensation and through the hands of a person dedicated to the service of God.

Today a kosher poultry-processing plant may hire, perhaps, a hundred *shochtim.* Not one customer ever sees their ceremonial acts or functional skills. The screeching, squawking chickens are herded into the plant, and leave as frozen "food products," attractively wrapped in plastic bags for display at supermarket counters throughout the country. The ranks of vegetarians might be swelled considerably if one had to watch a creature being killed before one could eat of its flesh.

In earlier days it was the prerogative of any normal adult who raised his own animals to slaughter them according to the laws of *shechita.* For the paschal sacrifice, one could slaughter a lamb from his own flock. These experiences gave one immediate knowledge of the fact of death which transforms living creatures into food. A woman was as well-qualified as a man, in principal, if not in physical strength, to perform the acts of *shechita.* (Among the Jews of Italy, this question arose several hundred years ago when men stayed in the cities while their families vacationed in the Alps. Rabbi Chaim Yosef Azulai of Livorno wrote a responsum stating that women did indeed have the right to perform *shechita.*)

Our forefathers were a pastoral people. Raising animals for food was their way of life. Not only did they eat meat, they drank water and wine from leather flasks, they lived in tents and wore clothes made from skins and sewed together with bones and sinews. They read from a Torah written on parchment, used a ram's horn as a *shofar,* and said their morning prayers with leather *tefillin.* Not surprisingly, the Temple worship of this pastoral people included offerings of their best animals to God. Perhaps the best defense of this ritual is that it replaced human sacrifice, as the story of the binding of Isaac so clearly suggests. Agricultural offerings (vegetarian offerings!) also had their place on the Temple altar-- *terumah, challah,* flour mixed with oil, and wine.

How remarkable that a pastoral people should give the world a vision of a time of Creation when there was no eating of meat, and of a time of the Messiah when "the lion will eat straw like the ox" (when all the world would be vegetarian?). The compassion with which a shepherd was expected to treat his animals was implied in the description of God as a shepherd ("The lord is my shepherd....") and as One whose mercies extend to all His creatures.

Clearly, our forefathers were not only meat consumers; as a pastoral people they were also meat-producers. Does this fact make the practice of vegetarianism a stain upon the memory of our forefathers? Some well-meaning people apparently think so, and I recall with deep regret once reading a *teshuvah* by a young *possek* opposing vegetarianism as a Jewish option. Our forefathers also practised polygamy. Are we ashamed to recall that Abraham had two wives because in today's Western world he would be called a bigamist? Vegetarianism is a response to *today's* world--medical, scientific, economic. Meat-eating, like polygamy, fit into an earlier stage of human history. Unlike polygamy, meat-eating is still the dominant practice in the world around us, but vegetarianism is surely a foretaste of life on earth in generations ahead.

The adoption of vegetarianism does not imply that all other food customs are "bad," any more than adherence to monogamy makes polygamy "bad." In Jewish thought, the world is too complex and subtle to compartmentalize and label sacred and profane, mundane and spiritual, good and bad. A

Talmudic midrash goes: "Let not a man say, 'I do not like the flesh of swine.' On the contrary, he should say, 'I like it but must abstain, seeing that the *Torah* has forbidden it.'" (*Sifre* 11-22).

The traditionalist argues that in Jewish life the eating of meat is not only permitted, it is regarded as a *mitzvah*. One *must* celebrate the Sabbath with the eating of fish, fowl, and meat. I recall the thought of Rabbi Israel Salanter, that the sages set down this rule for the benefit of the poor, who depended upon the *kupat ha'kahal* to appease their hunger. Thus were the administrators of *zedakah* obliged to provide the needy with what was considered substantial food, at least once a week.

There were always Hasidim who tasted meat only on Sabbath and holidays, and at all other times abstained from meat-eating because, they claimed, they were not in the proper state of consciousness to eat in the manner of Temple priests. Only on the Sabbath--when "the righteous eat to satisfy the soul" (Proverbs 13:35)--do they permit themselves the eating of meat.

Vegetarian practices occur elsewhere in traditional life. Many *ba'ale teshuvah,* penitent, abstain from eating anything that comes from a living creature, and this includes milk, cheese, and eggs, as well as meat. So too it was the custom of Rav Kook's disciple Nazir not to eat of anything that came of a living creature.

The Laws of Moses called upon the Hebrew tribes to become a holy people, and therefore to eat only what befits a holy people; not to defile their bodies, as one would not defile a Temple. Christianity rejected the Mosaic laws with the words that what is important is not what goes into the mouth but what comes out of it. But, alas, we have lived to see the day when both the scientific community and the public at large are indeed concerned about what goes into the mouth--tobacco smoke that may cause cancer of the lungs, over-refined foods that may lead to cancer of the colon, growth-accelerators that may cause cancer in other parts of the body. We now read the words of Leviticus with a new consciousness: "Be ye a holy people. Do not defile yourself."

There is a painful incongruity in the idea of a halakhic authority inhaling deeply on a cigarette as he ponders the question of *kashrut*. Can a substance at the same time be kosher and dangerous to health? This is a question that will not go away, a question that asks our scholars to get in touch with the new consciousness about food and health.

This gap between our religious community and the new food-awareness is illustrated to me by the experience of a young man who became a *ba'al teshuvah* and moved into a traditional Jewish neighborhood to make it easier for him to observe the *kashrut* laws. He complained to me that in his adopted surroundings there were no natural food stores, and there was less interest in matters of nutrition--virtually no concern about the overconsumption of refined sugar and flour, eggs, and saturated fats. There even seemed to be less awareness of what it means to eat from the yield of nature. He asked, "Why can't Torah help me reach a high level of food consciousness?"

Surely Torah does support the interest of many young people of today in nutrition in general, and in vegetarianism in particular....

Thou Shalt Eat Vegetables
Rabbi Harold M. Schulweis

The lady next to me at the non-kosher banquet ordered roast beef, and I, a veteran "fishertarian," ordered fish. A soulless fillet of sole appeared on my plate, which I quickly smothered with ketchup, a condiment that has saved me from many a culinary disaster.

Toying listlessly with my dried sole, I observed my neighbor enjoying a succulent roast. She sought to console me. "You know, Rabbi, I really like fish better than meat." I asked her whether she wished to exchange plates. She declined. A little later she said, "Do you know, Rabbi, my mother kept kosher." I responded, "Mine, too." We struck up an immediate kinship of maternal *kashrut.* Then she added, "You know, Rabbi, fish is healthier than meat." I countered, "Except for the mercury count."

She made me think. How do modern Jews relate to *kashrut?* Keeping kosher is widely publicized. The first Hebrew letters I ever saw in the marketplace were on the panes of butcher shops and restaurants. *Kashrut* has endowed us with a considerable vocabulary--*treif, glatt kosher, milchig, fleishig, pareve, shochet, chalif, treibern.* The Torah, the Talmud, and the Shulchan Aruch devote much attention to the subject. Yet, despite its prominent place in our sacred literature, there is something trivializing about keeping kosher in the minds of many Jews. Some have dubbed it, "kitchen theology," a kind of "pots and pantheism."

In the third century Rav asked rhetorically, "What difference does it make to God whether one eats unclean or clean substance...whether one slaughters from the throat or the nape?" His answer: the reason for keeping kosher is to refine people.

The failure of *kashrut* to capture the imagination of the modern Jew reflects a failure to communicate the moral philosophy and poetry of this time-honored practice. Essentially, *kashrut* has to do with the way we understand nature and human nature. *Kashrut* reflects our ecological conscience. In the Book of Genesis, we are taught that God is the life of the universe and, therefore, life is sacred. God formed and shaped it all--from herb-yielding seeds to fruit trees, the waters swimming with living creatures to the fowl flying above, the cattle and beasts to human beings.

As a human being, I am not only part of but a custodian of nature. God has commanded me to multiply and be fruitful, to fill the earth and rule over the fish of the sea, the birds of the sky, and all living things. The Bible calls me *nefesh*, which some biblical scholars translate as throat--through which food and drink and air pass and give me life. As part of nature I take in nutrients to live. God said: "I give you every seed bearing plant that is upon all the earth and every tree that has seed bearing fruit they shall be yours for food. And to every breath of the earth and to every fowl of the air and to everything that creepeth upon the earth wherein there is a living soul I have given every green herb for food" (Gen. 1:29).

Set before us is the ideal of creation, God's original intention: a world of herbivorous animals, a vegetarian universe. That ideal reappears in the vision of the Prophet Isaiah, who imagines the world at the end of history transformed from carnivorous to herbivorous living: "the wolf shall dwell with the lamb, the leopard lie down with the kid, the calf and the beast of prey together, and a little child shall herd them. The cow and the bear shall graze, their young shall lie down together, and the lion, like the ox, shall eat straw" (Isaiah 11:6). The optimal vision of creation is thus embodied in a vegetarian diet.

But the Torah is not a book of ideals. The Torah reflects the constant struggle between the ideal and the real, between the vision and the facts. In the Bible God discovers the powerful, instinctive drives of human beings, their appetite for blood, nature raw in tooth and claw. In the wilderness after the Exodus, the former slaves are bored with coriander seed, the vegetarian manna which falls from heaven. "Give us flesh," they demand. Angry at this carnivorous obsession, God declares: "Ye shall not eat [flesh] one day, nor two days, nor five days, neither ten days, nor twenty days but a whole month, until it comes out at your nostrils and be loathsome unto you" (Numbers 11:19-20).

Nevertheless, God concedes to the imperfections of human nature, bending the ideal to the real. And so God re-parents with human beings and enters into a second covenant: "Every moving thing that lives shall be for food for you as the green herb have I given you all. Only flesh with the life thereof which is the blood thereof shall ye not eat" (Gen. 9:3-4).

In this covenantal concession to the carnivorous character of the human being, God is saying, if you must eat meat, do so with awareness that you are taking the life of another. If you must take the life of another, do so with compassion. The first primordial law of *kashrut* is *ever min ha-chai,* you shall not cut a limb from a live animal--a revolutionary notion in an age of scarcity without the technology to preserve meat. Against the pragmatics of pagan culture, the Torah taught pity for the sentient creature.

A revulsion toward blood is evident throughout our biblical and rabbinic tradition. We are taught that life is holy, life is in the blood. When beasts or birds are slaughtered, the blood must be poured upon a bed of dust and covered with dust. The message is clear: hide your shame and remember-- you are not dealing with an inanimate object but with a living being.

Life is inviolable. To bring unnecessary pain to life is to desecrate God, the Life of the universe. Out of this profound sentiment laws and traditions arose to reduce the grief caused to animals under our control. We are instructed to master the animal world but to do so with kindness. "Thou shalt not muzzle the ox when he treadeth out the corn" (DT. 25:4). In other words, do not muzzle the ox when he is plowing and in hunger seeks to graze, to which the Shulchan

Aruch adds: "You must not frighten the ox. It is prohibited to stand on the side of the road with a lion to frighten the animal to work hard and not to graze in the field" (IV: 186).

We are also taught to chase away a mother bird so that it does not see the plunder of her eggs. Maimonides says: "The love and tenderness of the mother for her young ones is not produced by reasoning but by imagination; animals feel grief, feel love, and attachment to their young. If the law provides that grief should not be caused to cattle and birds, how much more careful must we be that we should not cause grief to our fellow man."

The moral intuition that it is wrong to kill a living creature is woven into the customs of our people. We have no blessings for leather shoes or fur coats because they are derived from the killing of living beings for purposes other than food. On Yom Kippur many observant Jews do not wear leather; how can we pray for life and ask for forgiveness of sins while wearing articles made from the skins of slaughtered animals?

The Torah thrice forbids "seething the kid in its mother's milk" in protest to common pagan practice. Jewish conscience recoils at the thought of boiling a kid in its mother's milk, so the rabbis extended the law to encompass all dairy and meat products. Thus, this fundamental law of *kashrut* is at its core an expression of compassion for all of God's creation.

Humanitarian Slaughtering

Similarly, a refined humanitarian notion underlies the basic laws of *shechitah* (slaughtering). If one must destroy an animal's life, it should be done as painlessly as possible. The *shochet* (ritual slaughterer) must learn to avoid *shehiya,* the delay in wielding the knife that severs the jugular vein. He must maintain his knife razor-sharp, smooth and free from notches.

A rabbinic anecdote tells of a new shochet who was to replace the beloved old shochet who had passed. They tested the new shochet and someone asked "How did he do?" One of the men sighed. "What's the matter? Didn't he recite the prayers?" "He did." "Didn't he sharpen the knife?" "He did."

"Didn't he moisten the blade?" "He did." "What was wrong then? "Well," the man said, "our old *shochet* used to moisten the blade with his tears."

Kashrut, Morality, and Health

Beyond moral principles, there is a relationship between *kashrut* and health. The rabbis insisted that preventing illness takes precedence over ritual observance. How then can I read medical literature and not consider how diet affects my body? In 1961, the *Journal of the American Medical Association* reported that 97% of heart disease can be prevented by a vegetarian diet. In 1982 a doctor representing the National Cancer Institute pointed out that "changing the way we eat could offer some protection against cancer." And in April, 1995, *The New York Times* reported that, according to a new study at Harvard Medical School, middle-aged men who eat plenty of fruits and vegetables are significantly less likely than other men to suffer strokes years later. Similar findings have previously been reported among women.

We may think of ourselves as carnivores, but perhaps we were not meant to eat meat. Dr. William Clifford Roberts, editor-in-chief of the *American Journal of Cardiology,* writes: "When we kill animals to eat them, they end up killing us because their flesh, which contains cholesterol and saturated fat, was never intended for human beings who are naturally herbivorous." Is this nature's revenge?

Supermarket-bound animals are kept alive and fattened by the continuous administration of tranquilizers, hormones, antibiotics, and thousands of other drugs. Federal law does not require that these drugs be included on package labels. Thousands of animal drugs are currently in use, and some 90% of them have not been approved by the FDA. We enjoy the healthy red look of dead meat because of a process known as "culinary embalming"--adding nitrites and sodium sulphate to mask the natural decay of flesh.

Making Changes

The time has come for committed Jews to consider that both the moral thrust of *kashrut* and its health significance point to a vegetarian diet, a culinary choice that responds both to the ideal and the real of *Torah* in our lives. As I have gradually eliminated almost all meat from my diet, I know it can be done.

An incremental move towards *kashrut* can begin with eliminating from our menus veal (made from tethered anemic calves) and paté de foie gras (made from the livers of force-fed geese). They are *treif;* it is not kosher to feast on the tortured.

Another way to increase our consciousness about *kashrut* is to make Shabbat a vegetarian day, especially as it is our day of tranquility and harmony with nature. In addition, I recommend that we eat vegetarian meals at our Passover seders. After the destruction of the Temple, roasted meat was prohibited at the seder meal, to avoid the appearance that the home table was being substituted for the Temple, where animals were ritually slaughtered. Consider the new meaning assigned to the song of the one kid: "Then a slaughterer came and slaughtered the ox that drank the water that put out the fire that burned the stick that beat the dog that bit the cat that ate the kid that father bought for two zuzim. Then the angel of death came and slew the slaughterer that slaughtered the ox....Then the Holy One, blessed be He, came and smote the angel of death that slew the slaughterer that slaughtered the ox."*

Will we help the Holy One stay the hand of the angel of death?

---

*Ed. note: The reference is to a traditional Passover song.

"I Know I Shouldn't, But I Do It Anyway"

Rabbi Noach Valley
New Year's Message For The Year 5753 (1992)

A traditional rabbi fulfilled his life-long dream of making *aliyah* to Israel. He was serenely happy to be in the Holy land on Yom Kippur. So it came as a shock to him when he saw a young man eating a sandwich near the synagogue. The rabbi approached the young man and said, "Excuse me, sir, you probably don't realize that today is Yom Kippur, our Day of Atonement, and a major Fast Day." The young man looked up and replied, "As a matter of fact, I do know that today is Yom Kippur." "Oh, I understand said the rabbi. "You must be a sick person and your doctor ordered you not to fast." "I'm in perfect health," replied the young man. The rabbi smiled uneasily and looked up toward the sky saying, "*Rebono shel olam*---Master of the Universe---what a remarkable land this is! Here in Israel a Jew would rather admit that he is a transgressor than tell a lie!" The young man smiled and interrupted, "But rabbi, you see, I'm not a Jew." The rabbi breathed a sigh of relief and said, "*Nokh besser.*"

It is a known fact that many Jews ignore the Fast Day and eat on Yom Kippur. They admit to themselves that they are doing the wrong thing by not fasting, but they do it anyway. This is an example of what is called in psychology, cognitive dissonance, a major theory first promulgated 32 years ago by a leading social scientist name Leon Festinger. According to him, cognitive dissonance occurs when two simultaneously held thoughts, opinions or beliefs, do not fit together or are inconsistent.

A very common example of this is the person who believes that cigarette smoking causes cancer, but continues to smoke anyway. He might rationalize by telling himself that he doesn't inhale completely, or that smoking calms his nerves and, therefore, is of some benefit to him.

Another example is the unfaithful husband who knows that adultery is wrong, but still cheats on his wife. The philanderer could either leave his mistress or he could rationalize by telling himself that he isn't really being unfaithful, because he doesn't love the other woman or because his wife doesn't understand him.

The person who eats on Yom Kippur might argue that although it's wrong, he waited until the late afternoon before eating or that eating helped get rid of his bad headache and, therefore, enabled him to stay in synagogue for a longer period of the day. The person who doesn't attend synagogue all year might justify his absence by claiming that he can pray at home-- although he probably never does--or by finding fault with shul-goers with whom he does not wish to associate.

The person who eats improperly--with fried and fatty foods and high-caloric pastries at every meal--might know that this is bad for his health. His rationale is his belief, stemming from self-delusion, that his gastronomical indulgences are only in moderation and, therefore, can't hurt him. The overeater-- the person who goes on eating binges--might tell himself, "Boy, is this food terrific-tasting. I can't stop myself from eating now, but I plan on going on a diet tomorrow."

A Chicago-based market research firm, the NPD Group, reported in 1990 on a survey it had conducted: "Among consumers who said they were most concerned about dietary cholesterol and fat, consumption of such high-fat foods as regular cheese, hot dogs, gravy, ham, pork, eggs, beef and mayonnaise was not affected. In addition, 84 percent of those most concerned about cholesterol and fat selected regular cheese as their top dairy product." Harry Balzar, the vice president of NPD, which conducted the survey for Weight Watchers Frozen Foods, said that people say one thing and do another not out of ignorance, but because they lack the desire to change their behavior. "People don't change," he said. "We want to change, but we can't." According to Balzar, people may be eating less fat, but they are still not following the United States Dietary Guidelines which recommend fewer meat and dairy products and more fruits, vegetables and grains. (*The New York Times,* April 29, 1992)

The only way to reduce fat in the average American diet is to reduce the amount of animal protein. Recently, the Physicians Committee on Responsible Nutrition, a Washington-based group, delivered a hammer-blow to formerly-held authoritative notions of what foods are important for and enhance human survival. This group proposed that the traditional four food categories: meat, fish and poultry; fruits and vegetables; dairy; and grains, should be replaced by fruits, vegetables, legumes (which includes beans, peanut butter and soybeans); and grains, making meat and dairy optional! At the same time, the United States Department of Agriculture also demolished the idea of the supposed superiority of the traditional four food groups by proposing a revised version in pyramid form. In this version, the greater part of the diet would involve grains, legumes, fruits and vegetables, comprising the three food groups at the bottom of the pyramid. A minor part of the diet would involve meat and dairy, comprising the two food groups at the top of the pyramid. At the pyramid's very tip are fats, oils and sweets, which are not considered a food group and should be used sparingly. It was felt that a pyramid that divides foods into five groups would serve as a primary educational device to facilitate the learning of nutrition by children in schools for years to come.

Our best hope for dietary behavior modification is with young people who will someday become adults because, in general, the current generation of adults in America still adheres to outdated and discredited principles of nutrition. A survey conducted in June 1991 for the American Dietetic Association showed that 62 percent of the respondents still believe that if a food falls into one or more of the erstwhile traditional four foods groups it is probably healthful and nutritious, despite the fact that the current body of evidence shows this belief to be far from correct.

Even though all surveys indicate definite changes in American dietary regimens, fat consumption has not diminished. Americans are eating less beef but they are eating more chicken, usually together with the fatty skin. They are drinking less whole milk but are eating more cheese and ice cream. Despite the proliferation of health education in the media and the fact that they should know better, Americans are eating more animal protein than ever. "Weaning Americans from a dinner plate in which meat plays the starring role is like asking a 3-year-old to give up a security blanket." (*The New York Times,* April 24, 1991)

"I know I shouldn't, but I do it anyway," the psychological principle of cognitive dissonance, may very well rule our lives and determine our everyday behavior if we permit it to do so. This holds true for Jews who eat on Yom Kippur and for people who, self-destructively, adhere to harmful, inadequate or non-nutritious junk food diets all year long.

The United States Department of Agriculture and the Physicians Committee on Responsible Nutrition have released to the media crucial dietary findings that we Jewish vegetarians have known for a very long time--that vegetarianism is superior to meat-based diets, that people should greatly reduce their fat consumption and drastically limit their intake of animal protein, and that fruits, vegetables, grains and legumes should serve as the basis of the American diet!

May 5753 be a year in which many more Americans take these dietary findings to heart and live by them and live longer and healthier through them, rather than offering mere lip service by saying one thing and doing something entirely different. May it be a year in which we do what we know we should do. May our vegetarian resolve be strengthened and may we all enjoy a year of life and good health, a year of all good things! *L'shannah tovah tikatevu.*

Glossary

This glossary is meant as an aid to the comprehension of the text for readers who may not be familiar with all the Jewish terms in this anthology. It does not give exhaustive explanations of the terms (which can be found in the Encyclopedia Judaica). Nor does it give explanations of the numerous names of texts referred to by the rabbis. It contains only terms which are not explicable in their context. Many of these terms have variant spellings, since they are usually transliterated. The most common spellings are given here.

Aggadah: The non-legal or non-halachic writings in the Talmud and Midrash, often folk lore material, legends, tales.

Aliyah: literally, "to go up": refers to the decision to emigrate to Israel.

Ari: acronym for Isaac Ben Solomon Luria (1534-1572), founder of Kabbala, a school of mysticism. Jews often call their famous philosophers, teachers and rabbis by acronyms.

Ashkenazi: European Jews who generally spoke Yiddish.

Baal Teshuvah: one who has a renewed commitment to Judaism.

Basar: flesh, or the meat of animals.

Chalif: ritual slaughtering knife.

Challah: sweet bread eaten on the Sabbath, originally the portion given to the priests.

Cholent: casserole of vegetables, beans, potatoes and prunes cooked slowly, often made for the Sabbath. (Non-vegetarians include meat.)

Fleishig: meat foods in the dietary laws.

Fresser: an "eater," one who enjoys food, perhaps a glutton.

Gedemptah: culinary term, meaning "soaked."

Glatt Kosher: refers to the "smoothness" of a slaughtered animal's lungs, and has come to mean "particularly kosher."

Hasidim: a sect of Judaism founded in the 18th century, which stressed spontaneity, joy, and dancing.

Karpas: vegetables dipped in salt water at the Passover seder.

Kashruth/Kashrut/Kosher: terms referring to the Jewish dietary practices; foods which may be eaten.

Kamenetz: the town in Russia where the famous 19th century preacher, Chaim Maccoby, came from.

Kiddush haShem: Sanctification of the Name of God.

Knesset Hagodolah: the highest Jewish court which can make legal decisions.

Kreplach: dough wrapped around a stuffing, like ravioli.

Kupat ha Kahal: charity, specifically feeding the poor.

Kuk: variant spelling on Rabbi Kook's name.

Midrash: interpretation of the Scriptures and of meanings which are other than literal.

L'shanna tovah tikatevu: common greeting among Jews at

Rosh Ha Shanah, like happy New year.

Maggid: a learned person, or popular preacher.

Matzo: the unleavened bread eaten during Passover.

Milchig: dairy foods in the dietary laws.

Mitsvot: plural of mitzvah/mitsvah, which refer to the commandments that govern Jewish life.

Nazeer/Nazir: those who follow the traditions of the biblical Nazirites.

Nokh besser: common Yiddish expression, "still better."

Oneg Shabbath: literally, "the delight of the Sabbath," usually a special Sabbath dinner or a table of sweets set for after the Friday night service.

Pareve: neither kosher nor non-kosher, like fish.

Perek Shira: A collection of hymns praising the Creator by the earth, the heavens, vegetation and the animals.

Possek: one who is qualified to render decisions concerning Jewish laws.

Rabbonim: plural for rabbi.

Rambam: acronymn for Maimonides (1135-1204), a famous Jewish philosopher.

Ran: acronym for Nissim ben Reuben Gerondi (1310?-1375?), Spanish Talmudist.

Rosh Ha Shana: the Jewish New Year, comes in the Fall.

Sephardim: generally Jews from Spain, Turkey, the Middle

East, and northern Africa.

Shatness: refers to those Jewish laws which determine separation: as linen and wool, night and day, profane and holy.

Shechitah: prescribed method of slaughter of food animals.

Shiva: seven days for mourning someone who has died.

Shochet: the person who has been especially trained to slaughter food animals.

Shofar: ram's horn blown on Rosh Ha Shanah and Yom Kippur.

Shulchan Aruch: standard code of Jewish law and practice compiled by Joseph Karo, 1565.

Succoth: Jewish festival "of booths" in the Fall.

Tanach/Tanakh: acronym for the Jewish Bible, based on the first letters of Torah, Neviim, Ketuvim, or the Pentateuch, Prophetic writings and Hagiographa.

Tefillin: phylacteries worn at the weekday morning service.

Terumah: a portion of the heave-offering or harvested grain given to the priests.

Treif: not kosher.

Tsimmis: a dish of carrots, raisins, honey and prunes, cooked slowly, often eaten on Rosh Ha Shanah.

Zeddekah: charity.

Zuzim: a coin.

Biographical Notes

Rabbi David Brusin is the rabbi at Congregation Shir Hadash in Milwaukee, Wisconsin. He teaches Holocaust classes at Lakeland College and philosophy classes at Marian and Cardinal Stritch Colleges. **Rev. Sidney Clayman** graduated from University College, London with a B.A. Honours degree in Semitics. He helped found the Guildford Hebrew Congregation, was a founding member of the International Jewish Vegetarian Society and rabbi of the Finsbury Park Synagogue. **Rabbi Stephen Fuchs** earned his Doctor of Ministry degree from Vanderbilt College. He is Senior Rabbi of The Temple, Congregation Ohabai Sholom in Nashville, TN; and past Chair of the Central Conference of American Rabbis' Committee on Inter-religious Affairs. **Rabbi Everett Gendler** served as rabbi to Temple Emanuel in Lowell, MA for twenty-four years, and as Jewish Chaplain and Instructor in Philosophy and Religious Studies at Phillips Academy, Andover, MA for eighteen years. During this time he and his wife, Mary, maintained a large organic garden.

Rabbi Arthur Green currently serves as the Philip W. Lown Professor of Jewish Thought at Brandeis University. He was educated at Brandeis and at the Jewish Theological Seminary of America, and studied under Alexander Altman, Nahum N. Glatzer, and Abraham Joshua Heschel. He is both a historian of Jewish religion and a theologian, and views his work as a bridge between these two disciplines. He served as Dean and as President of the Reconstructionist Rabbinical College, and is the author of <u>Tormented Master: A Life of Rabbi Nahman of Bratslav</u>; <u>Seek my Face, Speak My Name: A Contemporary Jewish Theology;</u> and <u>Keter: The Crown of God in Early Jewish Mysticism</u>. **Rabbi Abraham Kook** (1865-1935) was born in northern Russia and came to

Palestine in 1904. He was Chief Rabbi of Jaffa, and the first Ashkenazi Chief Rabbi of Mandatory Palestine from 1921 until his death. A mystic, liberal, and humanitarian, many of his ideas aroused bitter opposition, and even the charge of heresy.

Rabbi Bonnie Koppell has served at Temple Beth Sholom in Mesa, AZ. since 1987, and as U.S. Army Reserve Chaplain, with rank of major since 1979. She is the recipient of the Army Physical Fitness Excellence Award (1994), the National Defense Service Medal (Desert Storm) and other Army Achievement Medals. She is also the author of many articles, including "The Prophetess Deborah" (The American Rabbi, Dec., 1994); "A Mikveh Ritual for a Rape Survivor" (Raavonot, Autumn 5753, vol. 9, # 1), and "On The Names of God (The American Rabbi, Feb., 1993). **Rabbi Emily Faust Korzenik** was ordained in 1981, and has been the rabbi to the Fellowship for Jewish Learning in Stamford, CT. for seventeen years. **Rabbi Michael L. Kramer** lives in Bowie, MD., where he has served Temple Solel for the last seven years.

Rabbi Sidney J. Jacobs is the president of Jacobs Ladder Publications in Culver City, CA, and co-author with his wife of Jewish Clues To Your Health and Happiness. He was the representative of the International Society for Animal Rights to the first worldwide conference in London on religion and the use of animals, and is the liaison between the rabbinate and the Jewish community of Southern California and the United Farm Workers of America. He was closely associated with Cesar Chavez. **Rev. Chaim Zundel Maccoby,** affectionately known as the Kamenitzer Maggid, was born in Russia about 1866 and died in England in 1916. He was regarded as an exalted preacher and had a great influence on the Jewish population of the East End of London. **Rabbi Chaim Chizkiyahu Medini** (1832-1904) was a renowned Sephardi rabbi, born in Jerusalem. At the age of thirty-three, he moved to southern Russia, where he founded many Yeshivot and published many works. He returned to Hebron at the age of 67, where he was appointed head of the religious court.

Rabbi David Rosen was born and educated in Britain, but did his advanced rabbinic studies in Israel, where he received his s'michah (ordination) and served as Chaplain in the Western Sinai. He was Senior Rabbi of the largest congregation in South Africa from 1975-1979, and Chief Rabbi of Ireland from 1979-1985, and lectured at the Irish School of Ecumenics. He is currently the Director of Inter-Faith Relations in Israel for the Anti-Defamation League of B'nai B'rith and the League's liaison to the Vatican; a member of Israel's delegation on the Permanent Bi-lateral Commission with the Holy See which negotiated the recent accord and normalization of Israel-Vatican relations; President of the World Conference on Religion and Peace, President of the Jerusalem Institute for Inter-Religious Research and Relations, founder of the Inter-Religious Co-ordinating Council in Israel, founder of Clergy for Peace and of the Rabbinical Human Rights Organization. He is also Professor of Jewish Studies at the Jerusalem Center for Near East Studies at Mt.Scopus in Jerusalem.

Rabbi Edward Rosenthal is Rabbi of Temple Bethel in Brownsville, Texas. He was the first Reform rabbi to serve full-time in New Zealand, and is a member of the International Jewish Vegetarian Society. **Rabbi Harold Schulweis** is the rabbi of Temple Valley Beth Shalom in Encino, California, and the author of For All Those Who Can't Believe. **Rabbi Zalman Schachter-Shalomi** is the president and founder of the Spiritual Eldering Institute, and founder of the P'nai Or Religious Fellowship. He holds the Rabbinic Chair of Aleph: Alliance for Jewish Renewal, the World Wisdom Chair of The Naropa Institute, and is Professor Emeritus at Temple University. He was Head of the Department of Near Eastern and Judaic Studies and Director of B'nai B'rith Hillel at the University of Manitoba. He has held academic positions at Brandeis University, Berkeley Theological Union, Academy of Jewish Studies, Reconstructionist Rabbinical College, and elsewhere; and has served as rabbi and principal at Congregation Agudat Achim in New Bedford, MA, and at Ahavat Achim, Fall River, MA. **Rabbi Noach Valley** serves at the Actors' Synagogue in New York City. He is the President of North American Jewish Vegetarians, and a frequent contributor to its newsletter.